CHALLENGE TO CIVILIZATION

CHALLENGE
TO
CIVILIZATION

INDIGENOUS WISDOM
AND THE FUTURE

BLAIR STONECHILD

 University of Regina Press

Printed and bound in Canada. The text of this book is printed on 100% post-consumer recycled paper with earth-friendly vegetable-based inks.

Cover art: "Spotted Thunderbird Healer" by Keith Bird (2010)
Cover design: Duncan Campbell, University of Regina Press
Interior layout design: John van der Woude, JVDW Designs
Copyeditor: Marionne Cronin
Proofreader: Rachel Taylor
Indexer: Sergey Lobachev

Library and Archives Canada Cataloguing in Publication

Title: Challenge to civilization : Indigenous wisdom and the future / Blair Stonechild.
Names: Stonechild, Blair, author.
Description: Includes bibliographical references and index.
Identifiers: Canadiana (print) 20230561497 | Canadiana (ebook) 20230561659 | ISBN 9780889779815 (softcover) | ISBN 9780889779846 (hardcover) | ISBN 9780889779822 (PDF) | ISBN 9780889779839 (EPUB)
Subjects: LCSH: Traditional ecological knowledge. | LCSH: Sustainability. | LCSH: Human ecology. | LCSH: Climatic changes—Social aspects. | LCSH: Indigenous peoples—Intellectual life.
Classification: LCC GN476.7 .S76 2024 | DDC 304.2—dc23

10 9 8 7 6 5 4 3 2 1

University of Regina Press, University of Regina
Regina, Saskatchewan, Canada, S4S 0A2
TEL: (306) 585-4758 FAX: (306) 585-4699
WEB: www.uofrpress.ca

We acknowledge the support of the Canada Council for the Arts for our publishing program. We acknowledge the financial support of the Government of Canada. / Nous reconnaissons l'appui financier du gouvernement du Canada. This publication was made possible with support from Creative Saskatchewan's Book Publishing Production Grant Program.

Dedicated to uncivilized peoples of the world—
past, present, and future

CONTENTS

PREFACE

I have had an interest in spirituality ever since I was a child in Indian residential school, where I experienced countless hours of Christian religious indoctrination. While biblical stories were fascinating, there seemed to be something missing as it related to my life experience, and the assertion that Indigenous people were savage did not feel true. This is called spiritual abuse by the Truth and Reconciliation Commission of Canada. It was not until I began working with Elders at the First Nations University of Canada that I began to learn the rudiments of our peoples' beliefs.

Challenge to Civilization is the final volume in a trilogy with *The Knowledge Seeker: Embracing Indigenous Spirituality* and *Loss of Eden and the Fall of Spirituality*. *The Knowledge Seeker* was inspired by the teachings passed on to me over the years by respected Elders, especially Danny Musqua and Noel Starblanket, who encouraged me to use my university training to articulate the nature of their teachings to a modern readership. *The Knowledge Seeker* found that there was nothing faulty with Indigenous belief systems—they were highly moral and effective. *Loss of Indigenous Eden* came about as a response to people who dismissed Indigenous spirituality as outdated, inferior to religions, or not relevant to today's needs. It identified that Indigenous belief systems have ancient roots and were universally widespread and viable for approximately 200,000 years prior to civilization coming along.

Challenge to Civilization: Indigenous Wisdom and the Future is the third book in my series on Indigenous spirituality. *The Knowledge Seeker* addressed the nature and viability of Indigenous beliefs, and *Loss of Indigenous Eden* examined how Indigenous sacred knowledge became oppressed, suppressed, and discounted. This book will demonstrate that Indigenous spirituality is not only still relevant but will be critical to human survival in terms of restoring balance with both natural and supernatural worlds.

Challenge to Civilization can be seen as a reinterpreting of the history of the world, but from an Indigenous perspective. *Loss of Indigenous Eden* reveals that civilization was an aberrant departure from Indigenous ideology and ways of relating to the earth. Civilization has since waged a relentless and often violent campaign to colonize Indigenous Peoples emotionally, intellectually, and spiritually. Part of this campaign has been to portray Indigenous societies as proto-civilizations that would have eventually trodden the path of human self-centredness, greed, and destructiveness.

As an alternative, I create the word *"ecolization"*—a state in which humans recognize that they are not the central purpose of creation, remain grateful for the opportunity to experience physical life, and continue to obey the Creator's "original instructions." In ecolization there is harmony with both the supernatural and natural worlds. Making such a statement is not starry-eyed idealism as it recognizes that humans were fallible and did make mistakes. However, they had the transcendent ideology, ceremonies, and healing strategies that enabled them to remain on the "Good Path." Instead, humanity today has taken control over the world and created artificial financial, economic, and technological living conditions that are steadily strangling the natural world and threatening our very survival. This book is not a matter of any brilliance on the part of the author, but rather a testament to the wisdom of elders.

The gravest error made by historians is to evaluate the entirety of human experience from the starting point of the rise of civilization roughly 6,000 years ago. In doing so, at least 194,000 years of Indigenous experience and wisdom is dismissed. This work deals with global issues and time scales that go well beyond just those of the contemporary era. It responds to issues of global critical importance by reaffirming the value of Indigenous knowledge and wisdom. Once they fully understand the Indigenous experience, scholars will have to re-examine the supposition that civilization is indeed humanity's greatest achievement.

Chapter 1, "Recalling Our Heritage," recaptures a world in which Indigenous Peoples and their ideology predominated. With a high degree of similarity in thought and practices and with strong connections to those still witnessed among Indigenous Peoples, humans saw themselves as the recipients of the benefits of creation rather than its central purpose. They acknowledged that they were dependent on the gifts of creation in order to survive. "Original instructions" were received from the transcendent world through prayer, meditation, dreams, visions, and ceremonies. What today is deemed superstition was their fount of insight and wisdom. This proved to be a successful model of survival, one in which the relationship with nature is seen as something to be nurtured, rather than nature being seen as a threat to be controlled or an asset to be sold.

Chapter 2, "Breaking the Bond," examines the emergence of civilization in small pockets of the Middle East approximately 6,000 years ago. Civilization itself is defined as "the stage of human social and cultural development and organization that is considered most advanced."[1] Its root "civil" implies a contract between humans to establish a way of life based upon human domination of the natural world. The achievements of humans became the only matters worthy of consideration. Any achievement prior to this modern lifestyle is consigned to "prehistoric" peoples, who are claimed to be devoid of knowledge or values. Civilization has waged an incessant war on Indigenous Peoples by discounting their ways of thinking and doing. But Indigenous Peoples had clear beliefs about their sacred relationship with other created beings and about their responsibility to act as stewards of creation.

Chapter 3, "Indigenous Apocalypse," corrects the misinterpretation created by the contemporary accounts of history. Civilization was born of a distrust of nature and a desire to exercise control over it. This ideology became increasingly powerful because of the rewards of commandeering nature. Civilized groups conceived of a new worldview and, along with that, created their own deities. Competition over control of resources led to conflict and war. The harmonious relationships and non-aggression values that characterized Indigenous societies made them prey to more technologically advanced and aggressive societies. As civilizations grew in power and ambition, they began to attack and dispossess Indigenous Peoples around the globe.

Chapter 4, "Knowledge and Wisdom," notes the difference in wisdom and moral values between Indigenous Peoples and those of contemporary society. In the Indigenous system, virtues such as honesty, humility, and generosity were not only highly valued but were also in fact the "laws of the land." Telling mistruths bore consequences at a spiritual level that were greatly feared. Understanding and imparting the deeper wisdom of words is an example of the difference between Indigenous knowledge and today's knowledge. Words can be used to confuse and divide and lead to today's fake news and the post-truth era, phenomena that can have disastrous consequences.

Chapter 5, "Natural versus Artificial," points to nature as the true base of existence. Indigenous interaction with nature is spiritual, whereas contemporary society has created a largely artificial world that involves finances, technologies, cities, and so on. Indigenous worldviews recognize that all created beings—plants, animals, reptiles, insects, etc.,—have their own valid existence. Allowing artificial human creations to dominate places our life-support systems at risk. Indigenous understanding strikes at heart of the materialist assumptions of modern society.

Chapter 6, "Dangerous Minds," questions the limitations of rationality. Modern education is a powerful tool of renewal but does not incorporate spirituality. Universities promote knowledge systems meant to further our secular lifestyle. Rationality does not adequately anticipate challenges such as climate and environmental destruction because it prefers to study rather than immediately stop damages. Wisdom, on the other hand, advocates preventative action to nip problems in the bud before they fester. Civilization has become the mental box that narrows our thinking. In fact, without higher guidance the mind can become a dangerous thing. Our failure to fundamentally resolve our problems is creating confusion, anxiety, and depression—in other words, mental illness.

The creation of our human-centred world has been a monumental project. Yet it is still only recent in terms of the breadth of our existence. Given the challenge to humanity's enduring for another 800,000 years, like the species that are most similar to us, a serious focus on survival needs to become the priority. Chapter 7, "Culture as Lifestyle," argues that cultural capital needs to be recognized as more important than economic wealth. Indigenous people had the strategies that would enable humanity to survive for such a long period. Social activities such as drumming and dancing created cohesion. The emphasis was on creating harmonious relationships, not only amongst ourselves but also with the environment. Today's educational, social, and economic systems require significant reform.

The current model of economics based upon capitalism and endless exploitation of the environment is not sustainable. Greed truly is the Achilles heel of humanity. Chapter 8, "Returning to Stewardship," asks, Is there not a way to live without destroying our natural environment? For Indigenous Peoples this meant nurturing rather than exhausting the flora and fauna. With greater environmental awareness and scientific ability to manipulate our physical environment, could we shift our lifestyle to be more considerate of the natural world?

As Chapter 9, "Needing Allies," notes, Indigenous Peoples have every reason to be upset about what has happened to their world. Only their spirituality gives them hope and allows them to rise above the fray. However, Indigenous Peoples have minimal economic and political clout. Therefore, they must rely on allies who support the need to return to Indigenous ways, and are prepared to bring about systematic change from within.

The final chapter, "The Only Viable Path," contends that at some point newcomers to Indigenous lands need to recognize the wrongness of their ways and return to a more spiritual way of life. Indigenous spiritual wisdom will be the guiding light. Prophecy has foretold that Indigenous Peoples will show the way, but it has also foretold that if the newcomers do not listen, then the human world will end. It will take thousands of years to correct and turn things around, just as it took thousands of years to go off course with modern civilization. Elders point out that we depend on the world, but it does not depend on us. It is not the earth that is in danger of extinction—it is ourselves.

Many believe that the displacement of Indigenous Peoples and the creation of modern technological society, with all of its apparent wealth and conveniences, is the best thing that could have occurred and marks the pinnacle of human achievement. However, increasing numbers of people are recognizing that things are going terribly wrong, with climate change, wars, social inequality, and artificial intelligence, among other things. Indigenous Peoples all realized the danger posed by greed, which is known by names such as wetiko and windigo. This book questions the dominant narrative that civilization is in fact humanity's greatest achievement. I contend that it is not.

ACKNOWLEDGEMENTS

I begin by acknowledging Kise-Manitow, the Creator, and the gifts of creation provided to humanity, including intelligence and the ability to communicate. Elders have said that modern tools of communication, including books, are necessary to meet the challenges of educating a public often unfamiliar with the most basic understandings of Indigenous culture and spirituality. The Elders I have met in over four decades of teaching at First Nations University of Canada have been my mentors. In particular I acknowledge Danny Musqua and Noel Starblanket, both of whom have returned to the spirit world. I thank Elder Clayton Episkenew for his support and for praying for the success of this work.

I am grateful for the support of the administration at First Nations University of Canada, including President Jacqueline Ottmann, Vice President, Academic, Bob Kayseas, and other colleagues with whom I have discussed or consulted ideas formally or informally, including Jesse Archibald-Barber and Ed Doolittle. I thank my colleagues in the Department of History and the Department of Gender, Religion, and

Critical Studies at the University of Regina, where I am an adjunct professor, for their support. The late Dr. Paul Antrobus encouraged me to broaden the base of my research. Retired pastor Frank Armistead, a strong ally of our people, has made useful comments on the draft. I acknowledge pioneering scholars who have previously broken ground in this field of spiritual studies, including Vine Deloria, Jack Forbes, Antonia Mills, and William Lyon.

My command of the Cree and Saulteaux languages is rudimentary. Mastering all of the nuances of the language requires a lot of time. Having grown up in residential school and off of Muscowpetung reserve, I missed valuable opportunities to learn the nuances of our Indigenous languages. Spiritual terminology is difficult to learn, as it used primarily in ceremonial settings and it is still not adequately treated in dictionaries. I owe any appearance of fluency in my books to language experts and colleagues Arok Wolvengrey and Solomon Ratt at First Nations University.

My wife, Sylvia, has provided loving and invaluable support in listening to my ideas and commenting on my drafts. I thank my adult children Michael, Rachel, and Gabrielle for their indulgence and patience. My siblings Sharon, Bernice, and Jim, and my late brother Gerry, have always been a solid source of encouragement.

Thank you to the fine team at the University of Regina Press, including Acquisition Editors Karen Clark and Rachel Stapleton, who have stood by my efforts on my books on spirituality; Managing Editor Shannon Parr, who kept production on a tight schedule; copyeditor Marionne Cronin; talented cover designer Duncan Campbell and layout designer John van der Woude; and finally artist Keith Bird, whose inspired painting, *Spotted Thunderbird Healer*, has created this beautiful cover.

ONE

RECALLING OUR HERITAGE

. . . .

ORIGINS

listened with rapt attention as mosôm Danny Musqua shared sacred
stories with me. Mosôm is a revered Elder, who spent twenty-
five years at the First Nations University of Canada as a resource
and fount of personal wisdom and traditional knowledge.[2] He was
regarded by our peoples as one of those most knowledgeable about
the worldview and philosophy of our Saulteaux and Plains Cree peoples. Books and theses have been based upon his teachings and he has
been recognized with an honorary doctorate for his lifetime's dedication to Indigenous knowledge. As a child he committed to memory
many sacred stories from the Old Ones, the Elders. As an academic
I had developed an interest in researching our peoples' concepts of

reincarnation—or rebirth, as it is more properly called. I approached mosôm with offerings of tobacco and coloured cloth to ask for his teachings on this matter. This met appropriate protocol when seeking spiritual guidance. The questions would broaden out to inquiries about where humans come from before we are born and about where we find ourselves after death.

Mosôm began by explaining the meaning of the name of our people—the Anishinaabek, the proper name for Ojibway. Anishinaabe, mosôm explained to me, means "people who came from the stars."[3] I was familiar with sacred stories, especially those involving Wîsahkecâhk, our "Older Brother." Such stories are among the first heard by young children. They involve sometimes fantastical, whimsical, and often humorous stories of adventures with animals. One heard how the frog's legs became stretched or why the duck walks with funny movements. The stories also acknowledge how animals had their own conceptions of family lives and relationships. The stories were not to be taken literally, but rather were intended to embody lessons that could be learned in order to avoid mishaps.

These stories are entertaining and never fail to capture children's attention. Non-Indigenous peoples tend to dismiss such stories as fantasy, but they are extremely profound and are sacred to our people because they have been obtained through spiritual inquiry involving dreams, visions, and meditation. But to understand their deeper meaning takes a more mature period of listening, learning, and questioning. It is like peeling back the layers of an onion. As a child, one is satisfied with the stories involving animals, as this brings one's attention to how people are dependent on those natural relationships. But as one gets older, one may begin asking questions such as who Wîsahkecâhk really is and what our purpose for living on Earth is.

A similar example is the Christian story of Adam and Eve eating the fruit of the tree of knowledge of good and evil. According the biblical account, if they ate this fruit humans would become like God, but the consequences would be dire: "The Lord commandeth the man: You are free to eat from any tree in the garden [of Eden] but you must not eat of the tree of knowledge of good and evil, for when you do eat of it you will surely die."[4] Peeling back the layers of that story also uncovers a lot, as will be examined later.

I have had the opportunity to broaden my knowledge by learning from excellent researchers such as Antonia Mills, professor emeritus of First Nations Studies. Antonia came to speak to my class about the book she coedited, *Amerindian Rebirth*, which describes studies about Indigenous beliefs in reincarnation across the Americas. She trained under expatriate Canadian Ian Stevenson, who graduated at the top of his class in psychiatry at McGill University before moving to the University of Virginia at Charlottesville, where he established the world's largest centre on reincarnation studies, which I took the opportunity to visit.[5]

Ian Stevenson's fascinating initial publication, *Twenty Case Studies Suggestive of Reincarnation*, includes several cases from Indigenous communities of the northwest coast. Using rigorous research methodologies, Stevenson concluded that certain precocious children spontaneously and adamantly recall belonging to another family in a previous life. By around the age of seven, however, that memory dissipates. After the investigation of their descriptions, many of the children's accounts proved to be amazingly accurate.[6]

Of greatest interest to me in reincarnation studies is the notion that spirit is real and that consciousness persists beyond physical death. That life itself is a cycle is one of the most fundamental of Indigenous beliefs. I also explored other areas of research, such as near-death experiences (NDEs). Some people have experienced technical death, with no remaining heartbeat or brain activity, yet reported being conscious. Some individuals who have undergone this experience report floating above their body and accurately describe what was happening to their physical being while apart from it. Mosôm Danny recounted ending up in an emergency room after a trauma, leaving his body, and seeing relatives in an adjoining room.

According to prevailing conventional theories, the human body has been evolving on this planet over a period of a few million years. There have been several variations of this physical form, with most ending up as failures on the evolutionary tree. Approximately 200,000 years ago, something dramatic happened—modern humans, *homo sapiens sapiens*,[7] emerged. This creature exhibited the same essential physiological and intellectual capacities that humans possess today. It is said that if they appeared in a crowd today, they would not be distinguished as different. So, what happened?

Making sense of the stories that mosôm shared with me, I can only come to one conclusion: that we traveled to Earth in spirit form. Here, we were joined with the pre-existing hominid bodies that had been evolving over millions of years. Our consciousness entered into, and became the master consciousness of, these creatures. Mosôm had talked about spirit travel. So the ability to spiritually bond with these physical bodies was the last piece of the mystery. Mosôm often talked about the challenge of learning to control these newly acquired physical bodies and that it would be a difficult struggle. But they were the vehicles we had chosen for our earthly experience.[8]

The physical bodies we selected evolved physically on earth over millennia and are ideally suited for survival on the planet. But it would appear that our consciousness is very different. If our consciousness had evolved on Earth, as part of previous animal forms, why are we not more in harmony with them? It is becoming increasingly obvious how out of step we are with the natural world.

Indigenous origin stories from across the globe speak about humans coming from the stars.[9] Another interesting implication of this phenomenon is the question, If we are spirit consciousnesses that are newly and recently arrived on Earth, does that in fact make us aliens on this planet? Are we even like an invasive presence? In popular culture, much is made of the danger of hostile aliens invading Earth, taking over our planet and resources, and enslaving humanity in the process. Are we just projecting our own fears, as this appears to be exactly what we, as humans, have already done to Earth?

BEING INDOCTRINATED

As a youngster, I spent nine of my most formative years in the Qu'Appelle Indian Residential School in the late 1950s and early 1960s. The residential school system was based upon a reformatory model: Indigenous Peoples were seen as morally and intellectually deficient, hence education had to be laced with copious amounts of discipline and religious instruction. I recall the endless prayers that we were required to utter multiple times each day. Religion was the reason why the federal government entrusted residential school education to Christian churches.[10]

I had never heard accounts such as those recounted by mosôm Danny during my childhood. As a residential school survivor, I had been heavily immersed and indoctrinated in Christian lore. According to the Bible, the earth was created in seven days, with humans formed last. People were created in God's image, so presumably were the best of creation. Adam and Eve were placed in the pristine and harmonious Garden of Eden, but within no time at all they decided to eat of the apple of the tree of knowledge of good and evil. Defying God's will and wanting to be more like the Supreme Being, they were angrily cast out of the Garden of Eden and ever since have been under the scourge of original sin. But were Adam and Eve actually the first humans, or were they just the first to defy the Creator's will?

In the school we were fed an endless menu of masses, rosaries, sin, confessions, punishment, the devil, and eternal hellfire. In class we were taught about how Columbus and other explorers, the British monarchy, pioneers, and the Mounted Police brought order and civilization. Once out of the classroom and chapel, we faced a gauntlet of rules, punishments, strappings, detention, and bullying. Residential school was so effective that when students got out, they were convinced that our people were lazy, stupid, inferior, and inadequate. Many of us hated ourselves and succumbed to alcohol and substance abuse. Our wiser Elders counselled us to try to establish good relations with white people, but it is not easy to establish a relationship with an abuser who appreciates you only when you become more like them.

In this mammoth program of indoctrination, I was nevertheless intrigued by the knowledge being presented. I was fascinated by historical accounts of Romans, Greeks, and the kingdoms and empires of Europe. During our play, we preferred the roles of the cowboys who shot and killed Indians, as we saw played out on television. At the same time, I was left unsatisfied—something seemed to be lacking. I recognized that the way our Indigenous relatives were portrayed—as savage—did not ring true. The people I knew were humble, kind, and loving. Indigenous people always seemed to be treated differently.

Our behaviour was always suspect. The slightest failing, such as alcohol abuse or violence, was seen as indisputable proof of our moral weakness, while the same failing among whites was excused. There was little understanding or sympathy for a people whose entire culture, inheritance, resources, and worldview had been rudely ripped away from them.

LOST CHILDREN

Unmarked graves are a jolting reminder of the horrors of the Indian residential schools. In 2021, over 750 unmarked graves were uncovered near the residential school on Saskatchewan's Cowessess First Nation. The long-time superintendent of the schools, Duncan Campbell Scott, admitted in the 1930s that half of the students did not survive to see the benefits of their residential school education.[11] This tragedy is also a symptom of the Indigenous apocalypse, Indigenous Peoples having gone from living in a healthy world according to sacred ways, to having their birthright stripped away and being forced into a totally foreign way of life.

The graves sent ripples of shock around the world, and it is anticipated that many more will be found over upcoming years. This has forced the government and church authorities to pay attention. During a visit to Canada, Pope Francis, while not fully apologizing for the system, was compelled to ask for forgiveness for the actions of clergy members.

Pope Francis admitted, "When European colonists first arrived here, there was a great opportunity to bring about a fruitful encounter between cultures, traditions and forms of spirituality. Yet for the most part that did not happen.... Many of you and your representatives have stated that begging pardon is not the end of the matter. I fully agree: that is only the first step, the starting point.... I trust and pray that Christians and civil society in this land may grow in the ability to accept the identity and the experience of the Indigenous peoples."[12]

Subsequently, the Pope renounced the Doctrine of Discovery, claiming that it was later governments that abused the concept to dispossess Indigenous Peoples. But that position is disingenuous given how beholden the monarchs of the time were to the Vatican. What further proof is needed than that the first act in claiming lands was to plant a cross? One can question how much the Vatican, which is still a major apologist for civilization, fully comprehends the harms it has perpetrated on Indigenous Peoples.

RE-EXAMINING THE PAST

During my journey of nearly six decades as a student and an academic in the university system, I have had plenty of time to ruminate about the past. I reflected on my residential school experience and why it had been so necessary to brainwash Indigenous children. I vowed to go back further in history to figure it out. The difficulties appeared to start with the momentous collision between Indigenous Peoples and Europeans at the time of the "discovery" of the Americas. Still not fully satisfied, I went further back to look at the history of the Old World, where I quickly realized that Indigenous Peoples had also once lived.

What became evident in my research is the dramatic difference between Indigenous life experience and the profound lack of understanding of it by mainstream society. I wrote about this gap in my book *The Knowledge Seeker: Embracing Indigenous Spirituality*.[13] I studied the original Indigenous attitudes and sacred thoughts of our people, and found them to be very pure and ennobling.

Ernest Tootoosis, one of the first Elders I learned from, provided important context when he stated that Indigenous Peoples lived in the Garden of Eden and never abused the gifts of the Creator.[14] From this account I conclude that Adam and Eve were not in fact the first humans, but rather the first humans who embraced what we call civilization. Beliefs such as damnation because of "original sin" were not part of Indigenous traditions. In our view, Kise-Manitow was benevolent, loving, and generous. This stood in contrast to the God of the Old Testament, who threatened humans with punishment or obliteration if they did not obey his will. It was clear that, rather than facilitating spiritual harmony, religions were beginning to increasingly serve human agendas. As a child, one has little basis for questioning religious stories, so such ideas become deeply ingrained. Yet I had this gnawing sense that there was more meaning to life than what we were being taught at school. I couldn't put my finger on it, but that sense of wondering remained with me as I grew up.

In mainstream education we are taught that archaeologists, geneticists, and other scientists are convinced that life originated from some sort of biological soup. It is contended that we, as humans, are simply advanced apes—a sort of evolutionary accident.[15] But such an account never existed among Indigenous Peoples. The theory of evolution has been around for less than 200 years, compared to Indigenous stories, such as humanity's coming from the stars, that have existed for tens of thousands of years. So why are Indigenous stories not given more credence, or at least equal exposure to scientific accounts?

As I explained in my book *Loss of Indigenous Eden*, I became preoccupied with needing to understand the differences between how Indigenous and non-Indigenous peoples thought. Puzzled, I went to the library and sought out several books on the "rise of civilization" that

I hoped would provide some clues. What I discovered was eye-opening. I found that every book on this subject is predicated on one basic and simple assumption: that civilization occurred when mankind decided to rise up against and conquer nature.[16] As I pondered this, it occurred to me how contrary this was to the teachings that I had received from Elders. Humans, they told me, were the last to arrive on Earth. In return for being granted the privilege of experiencing physical life, we were to be humble and thankful for Manitow's gifts. Moreover, we had been given responsibilities: to respect all other beings and to behave as stewards, caring for our animal, plant, and mineral brethren.

In contrast, the Abrahamic Supreme Deity exhorted humans to procreate and to make use of the animals and plants. In essence, the biblical God had taken a radically different approach from the ancient universal wisdom and values of Indigenous Peoples. Instead of living in harmonious relations, humans were given permission to become masters and exploiters of the natural world.

The responsibility of living in harmonious relationships within this physical world is not an easy task. Elder Musqua said that it will be a constant struggle to maintain good and healthy relationships. Nature could be our greatest teacher and support for our existence. This is why we used ceremonies to keep us connected to and able to communicate with the natural world in a spiritual way. We did not worship animals, as some theologians have wrongly claimed.

Eventually, the allure of civilization, with its pandering to human-centred whims, began to compete with and wage an aggressive and relentless ideological war against the Indigenous worldview. The purpose of this conflict was to convince everyone that Indigenous ideas held no value and that Indigenous ways would inevitably and inexorably give way and evolve into the current form of lifestyle.

ORIGINAL INSTRUCTIONS

Some have the impression that Indigenous Peoples did not have any "law and order" to follow. This was certainly not the case. One difference is that Indigenous laws were spiritually inspired rather than "man-made." The Seven Laws (or Seven Virtues)—humility, bravery, respect, generosity, honesty, love, and wisdom—were the primary ordinances. They were even more strictly observed than secular laws and were rigorously enforced, as there could be dire consequences for transgression. Some consequences were of a numinous nature, where one would face misfortune, and others were enforceable by the community through, for example, banishment or even death. There was broad consensus about the validity of these sacred laws. As long as one followed the directions of the Creator, one had positive outcomes and did not have to lose hope for the future. Children learned from their earliest days about the sacredness of the world—how every created thing was alive and had spirit. Through stories, they gained a sense of their place in creation and learned about the Seven Laws and what the expectations were for their behaviour. Humility is one of the most foundational of the laws. It arises from Indigenous beliefs about our origins—that humans are the latest arrivals on Earth, that we are privileged to be able to enjoy the gifts of Kise-Manitow and need to acknowledge this through gratefulness. We are the beneficiaries of life—not its central purpose. Upon arrival on Earth, we were totally dependent on the animals and plants for our survival. In our belief system, animals, plants, and other beings are our spiritual relatives, and we refer to them as such in our ceremonies.

It is said that when the human being was brought to the earth, the Creator called all the animals of the earth together to ask them certain questions. The animals did gather and were honoured to be asked, and the Creator told them about the impending arrival of the human being. The animals were excited. The Creator told them that the human being would not be like them but would have certain gifts. The animals were told to keep the human close to them and to help the human when needed. The Creator bestowed upon the human being the gift of knowledge of truth and justice. The only way they can find these gifts are if they look inside their hearts, only the bravest and purest of heart would be able to do so.[17]

In terms of a natural order, we are mere humans, we are at the bottom of the chain and therefore need to respect our life sources, the plants and animals, in order to survive...Thus, in order to understand the Creator and spirituality, we must first understand Mother Earth.[18]

Much disdain was shown for our ceremonies in which there were appeals to animal guardian spirits. Indigenous Peoples worshipped the animals, Christian religious leaders claimed. However, this is far from the truth. As the latest arrivals, we looked to the animals and plants both to learn about living and surviving on Earth and also for help whenever in need of sustenance. After all, according to our sacred stories, the animals and plants could teach us. In return we were to be thankful and appreciative—something we do when we leave offerings after hunting or harvesting plants. We did not fear nature, but rather saw it as a benevolent gift and source of essential sustenance. This is not to say that there were not dangers, but animals, plants, amphibians, and insects all had a right to exist and each play their own role in the web of life. They just had to be respected.

The birth of humanity can be likened to the birth of an individual. An infant's initial experience and awareness of life is one of being overwhelmed. Gradually one becomes more aware of one's surroundings and becomes more capable of survival. But how one decides to behave in a new environment depends increasingly on that individual's maturity. One can continue to be respectful, or one can begin to abuse one's bounty. Today, humility is a rare commodity. We view ourselves as being far above animals and plants. They are not much more than wild objects to be domesticated for produce, harvested for profit, or kept as pets. Our attitude when it comes to the natural world is to dominate and control it. Sure, there are lovers of nature who claim that they would never harm anything. But does that attitude derive from a sense of spiritual reverence, or is it simply just a sense of physical coexistence?

Respect is another foundational law. Among other things, respect includes allowing other individuals and groups to do what they honestly believe best for their survival. It also means not invading the territories of others, usurping ownership of their lands, and exploiting their resources. Finally, there is reverence for the inherent right of every created thing to exist.

As a virtue, bravery was lost when non-Indigenous peoples saw nature as a danger rather than as a foundation for survival provided by the Creator. The need to dominate and control the environment meant the abandonment of faith that Manitow provided everything that humanity needed. These resources were to be freely available to all in the form of the commons.

It is hard to believe that a society actually existed where honesty, humility, courage, generosity, love, respect, and wisdom were the laws of the land and were complied with. Yet this was the situation in the Indigenous Eden of the Americas. This fact is never acknowledged by colonizers, who believe that such moral observance could never exist without the enforcement of written laws and police. Yet these virtues were more effective than the Ten Commandments, as they were intended to forestall the evils of dishonesty, disrespect, theft, hatred, and violence. Should transgressions occur, there were protocols to bring about healing.

A lot of non-Indigenous students think that Indigenous spirituality is similar to the New Age movement—no pressure, no rules, and no boring rituals. However, Indigenous spirituality is in fact rigorous and challenging. The level at which one engages is dependent on one's interest, maturity, and commitment. What European observers and historians failed to recognize is that pursuit of the sacred was a primary focus of Indigenous life. Industrious Europeans, who were looking for every opportunity for economic expansion and enrichment, simply could not appreciate the value of such a spiritual lifestyle. From their point of view, Indigenous Peoples spent too much idle time in what were perceived as worthless dancing and rituals.

INDIGENOUS LONGEVITY

Historians like to laud the longevity of "ancient" civilizations, such as the 1,000-year reign of the Roman Empire. But what about the longevity of Indigenous cultures that could persist indefinitely because of their life-enhancing philosophy and practices? For example, the Mayan culture is believed to have persisted for 4,600 years. Had it not been for European invasion, how many more centuries might it have lasted? Indigenous cultures sought harmony with their surroundings and avoided exploiting or overwhelming the natural environment. Such a philosophy promoted life systems designed to ensure abundance for future generations. There was a built-in mechanism for rejuvenation. Their cyclical concept of time meant that when an era of human activity came to an end, it was an opportunity to renew thinking and approaches. This could involve abandonment of entire urban centres that had overutilized their natural environment. Indigenous planning took into account long-term survival, not just short-term prosperity.

In Indigenous societies the focus was on respecting the spiritual bond with their land, rather than on aggression to take over that of others. However, conflict could occur, generally for defence or for cultural reasons, such as conducting raids as a form of ritual to demonstrate individual bravery. People were reminded that they needed to continually humble themselves in the face of supernal mysteries. With this humility, they did not need to rush to control their environment or compete against others for resources. Harmonious relationships with neighbouring groups were prized and were cultivated through shared rituals, dances, and practical measures such as intermarriage.

UNIVERSAL INDIGENOUS BELIEF

Indigenous beliefs existed in every corner of the world prior to the advent of civilization. In Europe, Indigenous Celts once occupied much of the area from the British Isles to as far east as Turkey, and south to Italy and Spain. Like Aboriginal Peoples across the world, their medicine practitioners, the Druids, used ceremonies to mediate between the temporal and spiritual worlds. They perceived that the divine was manifested in nature and that people were an integral part of it. The spirit that existed in all things was venerated. They also believed that humans reincarnated as part of the cycle of life. The natural world was not to be conquered, but rather was to be lived with harmoniously. Humanity was just one functional part of nature, and all elements had to work cooperatively together. Their sages, the Druids, had the responsibility of conveying the wisdom of their ancestors and keeping sacred practices alive. Their healers, called "wicce," were later portrayed by Christianity as evil witches. Stonehenge, a creation that predated the Druids, is indicative of an even more ancient worldview that took into careful account the movements of the sun and stars.[19]

The word "pagan," meaning peasant or country-dweller in Latin, was a derogatory term used by the Romans to describe those who were uncivilized and inferior. Pagans were in fact adherents to an Indigenous belief system. Roman officials went to great lengths to portray the Celts as barbarians in order to justify conquest of their territories. The Roman Empire pushed Original Peoples out of their lands, and their populations were decimated in a series of crusades. Today remnants of Celtic tradition can be found in Ireland, northwest France, and outlying areas in Europe. Other remnants of Indigenous heritage can be found across the world.

TENGRISM (MIDDLE EAST)

Tengrism is the original Indigenous belief system that spans areas of the Middle East from Bulgaria, Hungary, Turkey, and Kyrgyzstan to Mongolia. It was another Indigenous belief system since displaced by the ideologies of religion. The name originates from the Turkic word for its Supreme being, Tengri, meaning "Heaven." Tengri was viewed as the sustainer of existence, along with the spirits of nature such as earth, air, fire, and water, as well as ancestor spirits. Animals are regarded as having souls and therefore are to be respected accordingly.

Shamans travel into realms both above and below the earth seeking answers to questions. Through proper living, people could keep the world in balance. Elements of Tengrism, which exhibits characteristics of Indigenous shamanism and recognizes the existence of spirit in all forms of creation, survive in small pockets today.

Tengrism was supplanted by Islam in the fourteenth century. However, with the proclamation of the Turkish Republic in 1923, Tengrism experienced somewhat of a revival as part of the search for Turkish spiritual roots. Tengrism is identified as an ancient pre-Islamic tradition by historians, writers, and poets. In regions such as Kazakhstan and Kyrgyzstan, Tengrism continues to be embraced as the Indigenous religion. Tengrists perceive fundamental differences between their beliefs and those of Islam, where prophets, scriptures, dogma, and clergy can be seen as overly rigid and suppressive. Muslims have condemned Tengrists as infidels, persecuted shamans, and banned Tengrist symbols and instruments. Others recognize that there has been a fusion of beliefs, with Tengrism heavily influencing Sufism.[20]

DALITS (INDIA)

In 2012 I visited the Acharya Nagarjuna University in India. There I witnessed efforts to provide postsecondary education to Dalit people. Dalit is a broad term for numerous Indigenous groups that constitute about 125 million of India's population. Otherwise known as "untouchables," they were relegated to the lowest rung of the caste system by the incoming creators of that system, the Brahmins. It is acknowledged that, while the Dalit were severely discriminated against, they were nevertheless peaceful and reliable labourers who provided a strong foundation to the Indian economy.

History bears ample evidence that Dalits and most indigenous peoples have not taken up violence as a path of life. One would shudder to even imagine the consequence of Dalits taking up violent ways.... If Dalits opted to join hands with those that believe in violence this country can ever be governed at all. This country owes a lot to Dalits for believing in non-violence much before any religious doctrine of non-violence and any ideology of non-violence came into existence.[21]

Dalits recognized the natural life cycles of the earth, and that earth produces and nurtures life: "Her lifecycle is akin to the lifecycle of a woman. Therefore, it is appropriate to symbolize earth as a woman and as a mother.... Dalit spirituality believes that it has to be in harmony with nature and not to overpower nature through its machinations. The integrity of the cosmos cannot be violated by human folly as it is happening today in the dominant world."[22]

At the time of my visit, the capital, Delhi, was the most polluted city in the world. Indian government authorities were just beginning to recognize that Indigenous knowledge can contribute valuable wisdom when it comes to caring for the environment.

TAOISM (CHINA)

Taoism is referred to as the Ancient Way. It is the Chinese Indigenous belief system that revered the spirits of nature and rendered respect to ancestors. It preceded Confucianism, which today has become the dominant religion.

Confucianism, as an ideology, moved much closer to the embracing of civilization. It focused on the centrality of humankind and on how individuals and society are to regulate their behaviour. While retaining strong elements of ceremony, it de-emphasized connection to nature, and its rituals became more prescribed than spontaneous. Confucianism helped to lay the foundation for a society with a large-scale population:

> The indigenous spiritual traditions, including shamanism and local nature cults, were overtaken by a context of severe technological and political change. Taoism was part of this age of upheaval, offering a path of detachment and otherworldliness, while preserving strands of animist spiritual tradition.... An emphasis on simplicity and an anti-state outlook put Taoism on a collision course with the demands of higher civilization in China.... In contrast, Confucius (557–479 BC) embraced the state and the New World Order. Instead of longing for the virtuous time of the "noble savage," before class divisions and division of labor, the Confucian doctrine combined cultural progressivism with the abandonment of connections with nature. No ban was placed on the gods of mountains and winds, ancestral spirits and the like, but they were no longer judged to be central, or even important.[23]

As Chinese culture grew increasingly bureaucratic and techno-logically sophisticated, it suffered internal political and military con-vulsions. For example, the Manchu conquests of the 1600s came at a cost of approximately twenty-five million lives, and more recently, the Chinese communist revolution of 1949 and its aftermath resulted in over forty million deaths. However, China did not turn towards wrest-ing land away from foreign countries or forcing assimilation on others, as was the case in Europe. While countries with massive populations like China and India experienced internal conflicts, the history of warfare between them is sparse. There have been only three recorded conflicts, all happening during the 1960s or 1980s. While the barrier of mountain ranges is an obvious deterrent, it is also true that even mountains would not prevent the actions of a determined aggressor. Apart from conflicts and aggression stemming from Europe, which included campaigns to colonize both India and China, there was minimal interest in engaging in foreign hostilities.

But as a result of the invasion by European countries beginning in the 1840s and known as the Opium Wars, China was forced to devise a strategy based upon the projection of its own economic and military strength in order to fend off European aggression.

The Celts, Tengrists, and Taoists are only a few examples of Indigenous Peoples around the world who had deep roots. Having seen that an Indigenous world thrived successfully for eons, we will now investigate how Indigenous worldviews became overshadowed by civilization.

TWO

BREAKING THE BOND

FORGETTING ABOUT INDIGENOUS EDEN

t has been a grave mistake for scholars to evaluate the entirety of human history beginning only with the emergence of civilization. This approach resulted in the dismissal of 97 percent of preceding experience, including Aboriginal cultural and intellectual heritage. It overlooked tens of thousands of years of Indigenous knowledge and wisdom. In order to properly assess our cultural evolution, it is incumbent on scholars to fully understand the relationships that existed prior to civilization. This understanding can still be gleaned from contemporary Indigenous Peoples. History needs to be studied and reinterpreted through an Indigenous lens which spans the entirety of modern human existence, not just the period of civilization. Had that occurred, the assessment of what "progress" is truly about would be much different. This would have produced a far different verdict about the rise of civilization.

It is difficult for Euro-American intellectuals to appreciate that Indigenous philosophy and thought existed universally prior to the rise of contemporary rationalist society. These intellectual patterns were spiritually based and were the reason why people related to their environment in a respectful and nurturing way. Indigenous Peoples all over the world still maintain the fundamentals of their spiritualities and beliefs and are philosophically opposed to the exploitation and abuse of Mother Earth. Civilization eventually whittled away at these beliefs, surrendering to the Achilles heel of humanity—its tendency to place its own self-interest above that of the rest of creation.

THE IDEA OF CIVILIZATION

In 1965, a major study sanctioned by the United Nations-affiliated International Commission for a History of the Scientific and Cultural Development of Mankind and involving hundreds of scholars published its results. The study reveals the authors' assumption that human civilization arose through physical evolution:

> What will prove most important to remember is that our species did not only inherit from its past its bodily equipment, dominated by its subtly elaborated brain, but also highly charged emotional centres and all of the strange ancient furniture of the unconscious mind. Man emerged bringing with him hate, fear and anger.[24]

Civilization, as perceived by the study, is clearly predicated upon a rebellion against nature, including rejection of and separation from the natural world:

> While in many parts of the world, Europe among them, the hunters merely played the passive role of adjusting their habits to forest conditions, in some regions of south-west Asia [i.e., Mesopotamia] *men were inspired to counterattack against nature* and make the momentous revolution in human history that accompanied the domestication of cattle, pigs, sheep and goats and the cultivation of wheat and barley.[25]

Subsequent scholars who write about the "history of the world" and "rise of civilization" all continue to parrot this same interpretation. They write about how humans brilliantly began to gather near the rivers, domesticate animals, and aggressively cultivate land in earnest approximately six thousand years ago. The philosophy behind Indigenous approaches of respecting the validity of being in balance with plants and animals is exchanged for human control and economic development. Pursuing agriculture over extended periods of time, humans began to assert control and claim areas of land "as their own." A new type of human-centred "web of life" emerged. Gone is the idea that humans are the humble recipients of the Creator's benevolence, replaced by a framework where humanity is now in charge.

The word "civilization" is based on the root "civil," which implies a behavioural compact arranged between humans only. This makes sense as this system largely arose around the same time as crowded urbanization: a divorce from nature where groups of individuals are able to assert their power, not only over nature, but also over weaker groups viewed as weak competitors. This mindset of dominating nature and expropriating resources, and of needing to maintain control over the "uncivilized," become defining characteristics of civilization.

Ancient cultures prior to 6000 BCE do not conform to and are excluded from the definition of "civilizations." This suggests the need for a word to distinguish those groups that refused to follow the civilized path. A more meaningful word would be *"ecolization,"* which reflects the idea that the conception of society should be holistic, including the interests of all created plant, animal, and non-corporeal "relatives." Among Indigenous people, final authority always rested with the spiritual nature of creation, the interrelatedness of life, and the ongoing consultation with the supernal. "Uncivilized" is actually a compliment since it indicates those who did not betray creation by placing themselves above and becoming exploiters of it.

ABANDONING INDIGENEITY

Indigenous Eden once flourished all over the "Old World." Ideas of civilization spread slowly at first, beginning with nascent communities in the "Fertile Crescent" of the Middle East. Humans began to realize that they were able to exploit natural resources, be they plant or animal, with little or no apparent repercussion. It would be an immense challenge to document in detail the demise of the Indigenous world, but I have taken the first steps in my book *Loss of Indigenous Eden and the Fall of Spirituality*. It is certainly beyond the scope of one researcher, this author, to do an exhaustive study of all of the detrimental impacts of the "rise of civilization." However, it is possible to provide a broad view.

Modern humans *(homo sapiens sapiens)*, according to archaeologists, appeared at least as far back as 200,000 BCE. Their initial population was miniscule, at about fifteen thousand individuals, and they struggled due to adverse climatic conditions such as drought. But around 70,000 years ago they began to thrive and their numbers began to expand. Common sense tells us that these "primitive" persons were somehow capable of making effective decisions that enabled them to survive for millennia. Therefore, they could not have been unintelligent. What was the knowledge that effectively framed their interaction with the world for the approximately 190,000 years that preceded "civilization"?

PREHISTORIC OR INDIGENOUS?

Following Indigenous spirituality, these early people would have revelled in the gifts of the Creator, being abundantly respectful and thankful for their opportunity to experience earthly existence. In the earliest years of human presence, our ancestors must have felt so beholden to the physical world around them that they barely thought of altering their environment. Thus, for the first 190,000 years, humans attempted to fit with such perfect harmony into creation, there was barely a trace left of their activities. There was no domestication of plants or pets—the independence of everything was respected exactly as Manitow intended. To apply the term "prehistoric" to these groups simply because they had no "official" written record of history is unfair to Aboriginal Peoples. The insinuation is that they had few thoughts, and those that might have arisen were not of consequence. Indigenous Peoples had oral methods of keeping track of events and retained prodigious memories for such details. They had no compelling need to keep detailed records as long as they followed the path prescribed by the Creator.

EARLY WORLD POPULATIONS

Civilization is believed to have emerged at the first urban centre of Uruk, in Sumeria, around 4500 BCE. From the perspective of the Indigenous world, these people were, in reality, a renegade group breaking away from a long-standing worldview. Uruk reached a population of around sixty thousand individuals, including slaves. It became a premier centre for trade and was surrounded by a double ring wall six miles long and fortified by 900 towers.[26] Scholars believe this region was the birthplace of the patriarch Abraham of the Old Testament. The laws of Uruk were similar to Babylon's retributive Code of Hammurabi, which originated around 1750 BCE. It is apparent that the social dynamics of early civilization had shifted dramatically from those of the then-dominant Indigenous world.

Figure 1. Growth of non-Indigenous world population[27]

200,000 BCE	0 of 15,000	0% non-Indigenous
6000 BCE	80,000 of 12 million	0.1% non-Indigenous
1492 CE	60 million of 540 million	11% non-Indigenous
1820 CE	800 million of 1.6 billion	50% non-Indigenous
2018 CE	7.3 billion of 7.7 billion	95% non-Indigenous

WHAT IS ANCIENT?

In academia, one constantly hears the terms "Ancient Egypt," "ancient Greece," or "ancient Rome." Sumeria, one of the earliest documented civilizations, only goes back six thousand years in time. Given a span of 200,000 years, these types of social systems emerged only in the last 3 percent of modern human presence. Within the context of overall human existence, societies like the Sumerian and Egyptian are not really ancient, but rather are only relatively recent developments, placing them in the "recent past." Only peoples who lived during the previous 97 percent of time should properly be labeled "ancient."

Early Sumerian beliefs included deities associated with the sun, earth, water, wind, and agriculture. But spiritual activity was becoming more specialized and hierarchical, with priests mediating between terrestrial and cosmic forces. Their deities were becoming increasingly perceived as exerting impacts on the lives of humans. The first recorded wars emerged in Sumeria, and it should not be a surprise that they also had a god of war.

Along with an increasing onus on human responsibility for their actions came peoples' need to police their own behaviour. The Code of Hammurabi, the template for many of today's legal systems, involved nearly three hundred laws with what can best be described as an "eye for an eye and a tooth for a tooth" approach. For example, law 196 reads: "If a man destroy the eye of another man, they shall destroy his eye. If one man break a man's bone, they shall break his bone. If one destroy the eye of a freeman or break the bone of a freeman he shall pay one gold mina. If one destroy the eye of a man's slave or break the bone of a man's slave he shall pay one half his price."[28] Punishments varied according to one's gender and status. Such systems increasingly replaced Indigenous spiritual laws and placed accountability and punishments in the hands of elites.

Greek philosophical thinkers placed the values of their peoples above those of everyone else. The Roman Empire, great admirers of Greek culture, also legitimatized the slaughter and dispossession of lands of Indigenous Peoples across Europe. Historians argue that technologically advanced groups would inevitably arise and become aggressive everywhere, including advanced societies such as the Aztecs, Mayas, and Incas. However, it is those cultures rooted in the Abrahamic traditions that created the dynamics that led to human-centred acquisition of wealth and assertion of power, which has come to characterize so much of our current world. China, India, and other cultures also developed advanced technologies; however, they retained elements of Indigeneity and, while experiencing significant internal turmoil, did not embark on campaigns of world domination. Unfortunately, respect for and harmony with nature has declined as China and India respond to outside pressures for economic development.

REDEFINING LIFE

Classical Greek philosophers defined the world in terms of order versus chaos, the latter being what they viewed as uncontrolled nature. This included people who lived differently from themselves. Greek culture glorified humanity's intellect and accomplishments. However, while democracy is touted as one of their great achievements, in fact such privileges were extended only to male Greek citizens. In reality, it was slaves whose labour made Greek social prosperity possible. In terms of overall freedom, Indigenous cultures demonstrated more democratic and egalitarian characteristics.

The idea that humans are not born equal is endemic to Greek and Roman thinking. These groups were the first to feel justified in embarking upon significant campaigns to subdue so-called "uncivilized" peoples, eventually controlling over half of the then-known world. Aristotle, who is credited with creating the "science of logic," taught that one needs nothing more than one's mind, which makes one not only self- sufficient, but also superior.[29] Aristotle also espoused the dubious proposition called the "Theory of Natural Slavery." In his treatise *Politics*, Aristotle explains that a slave

> is anyone who, while being human, is by nature not his own but of someone else... he is a piece of property.[30]

Aristotle continues:

> They are in this state if their work is the use of the body, and if this is the best that can come from them....The lower sort are by nature slaves, and it is better for them as for all inferiors that they should be under the rule of a master. For he who can be and therefore is another's... is a slave by nature.[31]

The Spanish and other colonizers would use Aristotle's logic to justify enslavement of Indigenous Peoples around the world. Motives for slavery were not universally uniform. Emerging civilizations were most interested in controlling other peoples and their lands in order to extend wealth and power. However, in Indigenous cultures disputes were more likely to emerge from violation of perceived spiritual mores. The Aztec seeking of captives for human sacrifice is an oft-cited example. But it must be borne in mind that warnings had been given about this practice, which occurred during the absence of Quetzalcoatl, their deity of knowledge, and the resultant age of darkness.[32]

From the perspective of the Indigenous Seven Virtues, these values had been violated by the "ancient" Greeks. They had lost humility, believing that their limited knowledge and reasoning somehow gave them special privilege. They had lost respect for others. Love was not for others, but only for their own power and wealth. They were generous only to themselves, expropriating land from those who had been conquered. Historians marvel at their aggressiveness, believing it to be connected with courage. However, the courage of the Seven Virtues means doing the right thing, even when it is to one's own disadvantage. The behaviour of the supposedly superior "civilized" is something Aboriginal people could not fathom. Finally, the Greeks had lost wisdom. In their philosophical musings, they began focusing more on the material than on the spiritual. They lost appreciation for the fundamental importance of positive relationships. Like other societies of this nature, they would "live by the sword and die by the sword." Unfortunately, Greeks and Romans set the template for our current "civilization."

OVERRUN BY CIVILIZATION

Rome grew into an urban centre of around eighty thousand. At that point, like Ur, it began to display aggressive behaviour towards neighbouring communities. The mythological founders of Rome, Romulus and Remus, fought over power and wealth, setting a violent tone for Roman culture. Mars was widely worshipped as their god of war. Nobility and stature were obtained through the cult of manhood and the ruthless exercise of power. Romans began to intimidate smaller centres, forcing them to submit or be destroyed. After defeating their main competitor, the Carthaginians, the Romans set their ambition on eventually controlling the entire world. Subjugating weaker groups and forcing them to become allies became their primary strategy of empire building.

Rome was fully beguiled by materialism—fine food, clothes, public baths, and the entertainments of chariot races and gladiator fighting.

Like the Greeks, taking slaves was seen as justifiable and was wide-spread. These subjects were forced to be household servants, labour-ers, business employees, prostitutes, or gladiators. The Colosseum symbolized the cruelty of Rome's rule. It served to demonstrate how Romans wielded the power of life and death not only over slaves but even over wildlife itself. A million animals were stalked and killed in the Colosseum, eradicating species in some areas. Such actions contributed to the disappearance of European lions by the time of Christ. Drunk with power and wealth, Roman emperors began to believe that they were gods. The morals of Roman rulers degenerated to the point where intrigue, betrayal, fratricide, and matricide became common behaviour.

The Romans found the perfect combination of aggressiveness, mil-itary technology, and tactics to inflict maximum damage on oppo-nents. This unleashed a potent force never before known to the world of the time. In the way of Roman ambition lay Indigenous *ecolizations* that only wanted to defend their own territory. The Romans believed that all their conquests were just, and that they were actually doing conquered peoples a favour by bringing civilization to them: "when Rome conquered a foreign people, it did it for that peoples' own good."[33] They exploited the Indigenous preference to seek harmoni-ous relationships, entering into sham peace agreements. Once in con-trol, the empire would move in to divest the local population of its wealth and resources.

Rome's successor, the Holy Roman Empire, continued to wage aggressive wars against Indigenous cultures. By the Middle Ages, Europe had been witnessing the expansion of the Roman Catholic Church for many centuries. The church was fighting fervent crusades against both Muslims in the east and pagans to the north. This enthu-siasm for the vanquishing of the heathen would be carried over into its contact with the Original Peoples of the Americas in 1492. The estimated population of the "New World" at time of contact was 120 million. In contrast, the number of people in Europe and the Middle East, the centres driving the aggressive spread of civilization, was about 60 million, comprising little more than 10 percent of the world's population.

DESTROYING INDIGENEITY

The collapse of Indigenous *ecolizations* is consistently portrayed as having occurred because their systems were inferior. But were they in fact wiser, in the sense of spirituality and respect for human and natural relationships? Indigenous strengths lay more in peace-making and creating harmony than in devising methods to undermine and steal from "weaker peoples." The collapse of the Aztec world is often pointed to as evidence of how Indigenous societies were dysfunctional. However, the extreme of human sacrifice practiced by the Aztecs was recognized by their holy men as being an error that would lead to the destruction of their society. It occurred at a time of the exile of their deity of knowledge, Quetzalcoatl. They were going through a period of spiritual and intellectual darkness, and eventually the practice of human sacrifice would have ended.

Ecolizations collapsed not because they were inferior but because of their relentless persecution and dispossession by aggressors addicted to greed and lust for power. The Original Peoples could not stoop to the level and tactics of the oppressors lest they become just like them. All they could do was survive and try to heal themselves.

The "rise of civilization" has been accompanied by specific ideologies that extol human "virtues" of strength, beauty, intelligence, and superiority. Such discourse pervades European philosophy and religion. Its most recent manifestation, the "Enlightenment" or "Age of Reason," has elevated human intellectual abilities to the point where it is considered the ultimate level of achievement, and recourse to spirituality is simply dismissed.

Disdain for prehistoric peoples is part of a long ideological war by aggressor peoples to distance themselves from ancient Indigenous wisdom. While scholars are transfixed by the evolution of civilization in Mesopotamia and Egypt, where the attack on nature began, little attention is given to the millions of ancient peoples who controlled their appetite for greed in order to live harmoniously with their environment and neighbours. "Civilized peoples" looked down on tribal peoples, thinking they were controlled by nature and were foolishly weak. In Rome, Indigenous Peoples were portrayed as stupid and backwards. The only time natives merited attention is when they rose in defence of their lands and became labelled as "barbarians."[34]

CRITIQUING CIVILIZATION

Rationalists argue that it is self-evident that people would want to protect themselves from threats and that there is a right to seek security. But why did the natural world become a threat? In Indigenous eyes, all parts of creation were gifts of Manitow. The animals "willingly" supply us with food, and the plants provide us with medicines. Certainly, there were dangerous animals and plants, but they had a right to exist for reasons known to the Creator. People had to accept that reality and comport themselves accordingly. The ultimate sense of security came from the belief that the world was created out of benevolence and would provide all the necessities required to live. The more people distanced themselves from nature, the more fearful humans became of it. This led to the breakdown of the sacred covenant to maintain harmonious coexistence and stewardship.

Elder and academic John Mohawk pondered the dilemma of these developments:

> So there was something that happened in approximately 5000 BCE that caused people to consider the possibility of domesticating plants and animals. These people were settled in a place and they could no longer migrate to another place because that other place was already occupied. Here starts the kind of story we need to think about. There is a predilection in our species, you could call it our primate instincts, that has groups of us forever aggressively looking at the possibility of expanding and taking over and plundering others. From the beginning until now, the whole civilization hasn't addressed this shortcoming very successfully.[35]

In his book *Civilized to Death,* Christopher Ryan takes another look at the development of the contemporary world and how it compares to the Indigenous life it displaced. The story we are told is:

> We are descended from prehistoric ancestors whose lives were a constant struggle against starvation, disease, predators, and each other. Only the strongest, cleverest, most anxious, and most ruthless survived to pass on their genes into the future—and even these lucky ones only lived to the age of thirty-five or so. Then, about ten thousand years ago, some forgotten genius invented agriculture, and thus delivered our species from animal desperation into civilized abundance, leisure, sophistication, and plenitude. Despite occasional setbacks, things have been getting better ever since.[36]

Ryan then observes:

> There is no evidence to suggest the foraging way of life is less
> sophisticated or satisfying than any other—including our own—
> and having lasted hundreds of thousands of years, it is certainly
> more sustainable. I don't share the ubiquitous assumption that
> twenty-first century techno-sapiens are the pinnacle of biology, or
> that our species is progressing ever closer to some exalted future
> state....Foragers tend to see themselves as the fortunate recipients
> of generous environment and benevolent spirit world. The land
> is the source of all they need. This view is roughly the opposite of
> the narrative of perpetual progress, with its depiction of the natu-
> ral world as hostile, dangerous, and begrudging. Similarly, foragers
> tend to relate to a spirit world populated with multiple generous
> (if sometimes capricious) entities ranging from dead ancestors to
> elements of their surroundings (water, sky, wind and so on) rather
> than the single jealous, vengeful deity at the helm of monotheistic
> religions....To the extent the savages are or ever were noble, we'll
> see that it's because their societies flourished by promoting gener-
> osity, honesty, and mutual respect—values, not coincidentally, still
> cherished by most modern humans at a gut level.[37]

He is skeptical about the attractiveness of civilization:

> Our ancestors didn't abandon a desperate foraging existence for
> the comforts of domesticity. Far from a bold step into a better life,
> agriculture was a tragic, stumbling misstep into a hole we've been
> hard at work digging deeper, century by century, as global popula-
> tion exploded far beyond the point of no return....Judging by the

archaeological evidence, nobody was particularly eager to adopt farming. It spread from the Fertile Crescent through Europe more slowly than an old man in slippers, advancing barely a thousand yards per year.[38]

This new lifestyle can also be recognized as the fall from grace as recorded in Genesis: "And to Adam he said 'cursed is the ground because of you; in pain you shall eat of it all the days of your life; thorns and thistles it shall bring forth for you; and you shall eat the plants of the field. By the sweat of your face you shall eat bread, till you return to the ground, for of it you were taken; for you are dust, and to dust you will return.'"[39]

Contemporary society exacerbates disparities of wealth and power as people increasingly flock into more populous centres. Once wealth emerged, so did elite groups who made decisions about how wealth was to be distributed. Materialistic lifestyles teach one to hoard property and defend it to the death if necessary. But we are not hardwired for war—it is something we learn: "The worldwide archaeological evidence shows that war was simply absent over the vast majority of human experience."[40] The benevolence of the Creator was accessible by everyone equally, whereas the gods of civilization exhorted their followers to vanquish competitors. It is sacred law that Indigenous People should share with others, and one of the reasons why so little conflict occurred.

ECOLIZATION OR CIVILIZATION?

The majority of the world population remained Indigenous up until the 1820s, when they began to be outnumbered by modernized peoples. That era is also remarkable for a couple of other reasons: the embrace of rationalism, the industrial age, colonialism, and rapid demographic growth. In the mere two hundred years since human-centred approaches became predominant, the world environment has been severely stressed and its stability has dramatically deteriorated. Is there a way to chart the transformation from Indigenous *ecolization* to modern civilization?

"Eden" was clearly the home of Indigenous Peoples. Ancient peoples had begun to be eradicated with the beginnings of aggression in the Middle East and Europe as civilization emerged approximately 6,000 years ago. The war of militaristic cultures against ancient Indigenous Peoples, a crusade of civilization, would accelerate as European explorers reached the "New World" in 1492. When the "explorers" such as Christopher Columbus came into contact with the Aboriginal Peoples of the Americas, they marvelled at the pristine environment, health, robustness, cheerfulness, hospitality, and generosity of their hosts. But their instincts of greed and brutality were too strong to leave behind.

The cultural foundations of China and India, although exhibiting the features of civilization, including agriculture and advanced technologies, were far different from those of the Abrahamic traditions. They were advanced societies, yet still acknowledged the presence of spirits of nature as well as those of ancestors. Such cultures were closely connected to their lands and were content to remain within their own geographic spheres.

The megapopulations of China and India are recent developments. China's population had remained stable, between 37 and 60 million, for a thousand years from 2 CE to around 1000 CE, and did not exceed 300 million until around 1600. Its most dramatic and significant growth started around 1930, and since then numbers have ballooned 300 percent from 480 million to 1.4 billion today. The primary factors driving this explosion were influences from Europe, in particular the introduction and spread of foods from the Indigenous Americas such as potatoes, corn, and peanuts, plus the adoption of more advanced methods of cultivation.[41] Similarly, explosive growth of India's population is a recent phenomenon and the result of external influences. By 1900, India's population was 240 million. The greatest growth followed in the aftermath of independence from the British Empire in 1948, with population soaring almost 400 percent from 358 million to 1.4 billion today. A startling one billion souls were added over seventy years! The stamp left by British cultural, ideological, political, and economic changes cannot be ignored as factors.[42] Yet Indian and Chinese belief systems did not imply domination of the world's resources and peoples.

Populations in Asia, such as in Indonesia, can be difficult to categorize because of the complexities of migration over the centuries and the watering down of Aboriginal populations. Ultimately, the definition of Indigenous can be distilled down to a set of values. These would include spiritual values such as those of the Seven Virtues, as well as prizing healthy relationships with human and non-human beings, as opposed to lusting for wealth and power. Nevertheless, it is possible to outline broad categories, from those that continued to adhere to Indigenous "original instructions" to those societies that chose to redefine the world in terms of self-interest. This chart is not intended to suggest that societies inevitably evolve into aggressive civilizations.

Figure 2. Deterioration from Ecolization to Civilization

Incipient *Ecolization* → Advanced *Ecolization* → Passive Civilization → Aggressive Civilization

- **Incipient Ecolization:** The most original and purest form of human organization, characterized by closeness to, non-interference with, and nurturing of the natural environment according to the "original instructions." Examples: precontact North America, Amazonian "tribes," precontact subcontinental Africa, Australian Aborigine, precontact East Indies.

- **Advanced Ecolization:** There is sophisticated knowledge of and developments in astronomy, architecture, agriculture, etc. However, these remain primarily spiritually motivated activities. There is greater development of human-based institutions and large-scale settlements; however, these constructions are harmonious with rather than dominating of nature. In terms of their ideologies and practices, such societies are not pursuing the same path as Old World civilizations. Examples: Aztec, Maya, and Inca.

- **Passive Civilization:** Developments give increasing priority to human-centred activities and the natural environment is increasingly impinged upon. The philosophy of human centrality and control over nature has emerged but does not totally dominate human affairs. There still remain some relationships with ancestor and nature spirits. While there may be inner turmoil, there is no concerted effort to invade and conquer the lands of others. Examples: China, India.

- **Aggressive Civilization:** Philosophy is clearly human-centred and there is religiously sanctioned authority to dominate and exploit nature. There is licence to overthrow those deemed to be inferior and to usurp their lands and resources. Aggressive civilization uses military and economic advantage to dominate those whom they perceive to be backward and weaker. Examples: Roman Empire;

British, French and Spanish colonial empires; Nazi Germany; United States of America.

The domination by civilization and final demise of the Indigenous world would be exacerbated with the invasion of the "New World." Conquest of the Americas fuelled the amassing of wealth and brought new competition to see who could discover and exploit the world's riches the fastest.

THREE

INDIGENOUS APOCALYPSE

THE COMING STORM

While environmental conditions in the precontact Americas were pristine, life was not very good in Europe in the 1400s. People struggled to survive primarily on marginal crops such as wheat and other cereal grains. Childbirth was difficult and perilous, and the mortality rate was almost one third in infants and young children. Perils included malnutrition, smallpox, measles, whooping cough, tuberculosis, and influenza. Much of this was caused by poor sanitary conditions in overcrowded urban centres that had long become divorced from their natural surroundings.

Such unravelling of the human condition in the Old World was just the tip of the iceberg. Civilization had been taking root for thousands of years, and it showed in terms of the history of violence, warfare, and inequality that manifested in Europe. The unravelling of nature's paradise had been unfolding for centuries and this catastrophe was about to be exported to Indigenous America in 1492.

Apart from the impact of gold and other wealth, the introduction of New World vegetables—potatoes, tomatoes, beans, corn, and chocolate, among others—injected new life into the Old World. The new crops were less labour intensive to produce and also more reliable in terms of consistent produce. Improved nutrition ushered in an explosion in European population, rising from 100 million in 1650 to almost 600 million by 1950.[43]

Civilization has historically been built primarily on the backs of the "uncivilized." This continued to be the case with the invasion and occupation of the Americas. Colonization was a monumental human movement that involved immense amounts of effort, passion, blood, and sweat. The advocates of individualism, frontierism, and free enterprise may have believed that they were doing a good thing; however, the wisdom of these approaches were not considered over the long term. After Europeans arrived it took mere decades for incredibly abundant swaths of the natural world, such as passenger pigeons and buffalo in North America, to disappear. All were considered by Indigenous Peoples to be sacred beings that existed to provide sustenance. Their abundant numbers were evidence of the stewardship Indigenous Peoples had observed. But now, after a burst of prosperity lasting only a few centuries, personal social and economic well-being in the modern world has begun to plummet due to declining resources.

The 1820s were a tipping point. Trade and economic development were beginning to expand across the globe at a feverish pace.

Indigenous people were being decimated and displaced within their own territories. For the first time the number of non-Indigenous people exceeded that of Original Peoples, forming the majority of the world population. It was also the last point at which global population, at about 1.5 billion, could be sustained without overwhelming nature. A nexus of an unparalleled quest for wealth and power, colonial exploitation of Indigenous resources, explosive innovation in science, technology, and transportation, interspersed by outbreaks of warfare, was propelling the world into modernity. This period, romanticized as part of the Enlightenment and Age of Reason, in reality was the unfettered trammelling of the Indigenous world:

> Missionaries, explorers, adventurers and anthropologists have been consistently mystified and disappointed by Indigenous people's rejection of the comforts and conveniences of civilization.... There is widespread belief that noncivilized human life was just a desperate struggle for survival.... Lies can be repeated so frequently that they become indistinguishable from the voices in our heads: Civilization is humankind's greatest accomplishment. Progress is undeniable. You're lucky to be alive here and now. Any doubt, despair, or disappointment you feel is your own fault.[44]

> In reality, people were coerced and tempted into joining civilization... [providing] cheap human labor to keep the economy growing, workers to plant and harvest crops, armies to conquer and hold new land, slaves to build roads. Where population originally grew very slowly—doubling every quarter of a million years—now it doubles almost every twenty-five.[45]

Philosopher Thomas Hobbes placed the blame for Indigenous people's not joining in the plunder of the planet on their lack of ambition and industriousness:

> In such condition there is no place for industry, because the fruit thereof is uncertain, and consequently, no culture of the earth, no navigation, nor the use of commodities that may be imported by sea, no commodious building, no instruments of moving and removing such things as require much force, no knowledge of the face of the earth, no account of time, no arts, no letters, no society, and which is worse of all, continual fear and danger of violent death, and the life of man, solitary, poor, nasty, brutish and short.[46]

DIVIDING UP EDEN

Despite our everyday familiarity with national borders, something we are taught as a standard staple in schools, boundaries are in fact recent developments. The first border appeared between France and Spain in the thirteenth century, but most others developed beginning in the seventeenth century. It is not a coincidence that the establishment of borders corresponded with the era of colonialism and the dividing up of Indigenous lands. Borders became an essential tool for powerful civilizations to stake out their claims and minimize the potential for conflict amongst themselves. Territories of the Americas were claimed by pre-emption—the simple planting of the cross—before the "discoverer" even knew what exactly was there.

Britain assumed the role of a latter-day Roman Empire because of its access to and mastery of the seas, enabling it to efficiently exploit

Indigenous lands in Asia, Africa, and North America. The Industrial Revolution gave Britain an unprecedented ability to rapidly mobilize troops and weaponry to quell uprisings. Their technological advantage in terms of weaponry was immense, enabling them to easily terrify the Aboriginal people. The British also instituted tightly run governance systems reminiscent of the way the Romans managed their subject peoples. Schools taught modern topics such as English, mathematics, science, and, at advanced institutions, parliamentary governance and legal systems, all useful for propagating the new lifestyle. But the introduction of private property and banking are some of the most consequential changes introduced to the world. All of this was packaged and sold as "progress."

Many came to the Americas to escape religious or political persecution and claimed to wish to make a new beginning. But inevitably, they carried with them their Old World values and ways. Is it any accident that the United States Congress and so many other significant structures in the New World reference Greek and Roman architecture? The attainment of North America's vast, unsullied wealth, the greatest windfall in the world, gave rise to the most economically and militarily powerful nation that has ever existed. The United States of America became the new paragon of civilization.

EXPLOITING INDIGENOUS PEOPLE

Slavery is claimed to be a worldwide phenomenon that can be traced back to the earliest civilizations. Indigenous Peoples have practiced it with equal guilt, according to scholars. "Slavery" is one of those words that seems black and white in terms of connotation. How does one define slavery when it is connected to cultures that were more involved with spirituality and relationships than with economic exploitation and domination? In advanced societies of Mesoamerica, slavery was more connected to ceremony, such as human sacrifice. Others taken from their communities through conflict often had the opportunity to integrate into the new community, in effect creating a new set of relationships that gave that individual worth and integrity.

Over the centuries, millions of individuals, a large proportion being Indigenous, were enslaved through conquest, raids, or trade. Aristotle's philosophy helped to normalize the ability of civilized peoples to enslave those who were perceived as inferior. For their efforts to defend their lands, the Indigenous Peoples were labelled savage and barbaric. One thing is certain—those millions enslaved over the centuries did not abandon their previous ways of life willingly. Neither did they have an option to simply return and pick up their old ways. As a result, these individuals and their descendants became hapless victims of civilization. They became forced to pursue lifestyles divorced from nature and to adopt values not of their own choosing.

Between 1525 and 1866 around 12.5 million Indigenous Africans were shipped to the United States to perform unpaid labour. Of these, nearly 2 million perished on the open seas. Today there are around 42 million Black people in the United States, most descended from the original slaves. At the same time, efforts to enslave Indigenous Peoples were not spared. Between 1670 and 1715 up to 50,000 Native Americans were traded as slaves. They were regarded as not as compliant, however, and that, along with the hostility from the tribes created by the trade, led to the ending of such trade by 1730. A Brown University study estimated that, between 1492 and 1880, up to 5.5 million natives of North and South America ended up in some form of bondage.[47]

AMERICAN MYTHOLOGIES

My earliest childhood recollections took place in Montana and North Dakota. My mother Lucy had left Edward Stonechild, who, after coming home from the army, fell into violent bouts of alcoholism. She ended up having to make a heart-wrenching choice confronting too many who suffered from the devastation of colonization. Mom met an American, Louis Adams, and moved to the United States for her safety and that of us children. It was a sad descent for Edward, who in his earlier years had trained to become a Presbyterian lay minister. I reconnected with Edward in later years, when he had become a fervent adherent to Alcoholics Anonymous. Were it not for alcohol, he could have been a strong contributor to our community. He had a strong sense of the injustices faced by our people and wished that he would have been more active in bringing about solutions. His life was hard and he died early of a heart attack on our reserve, Muscowpetung First Nation, at age fifty-nine. While in Montana, I had the opportunity to visit relatives at Rocky Boy Reservation. "Rocky Boy" is a variant of the Cree word *asiniwasis* or "stone child," a spirit being associated with ceremonies. Today Rocky Boy is proud of its higher education institution, Stonechild College, founded in 1984.

As a scholar, I took an interest in how American history is portrayed. The United States merits special attention as it is today considered the world's foremost power and leader. Yet this nation has failed to recognize its indebtedness to its original inhabitants.

This relatively new nation is held up as an international example of human progress and morality. However, a closer look at the mythologies about the nation's origins and purported destiny raise a lot of questions. One can wonder, Why did European colonists believe that they could simply take over a continent that really did not belong to them? What were the consequences of arriving on the shores of Turtle Island without any spiritual relationship towards the land? Indeed, were the values and ways that were imported antithetical to those of the original inhabitants?

The colonizers saw very little of value in the Indigenous people, who were subsequently demeaned, undermined, and nearly exterminated. Founding Father Thomas Jefferson was not so tolerant or forgiving of those who were trying to protect their land and prevent its being wrested away: "If ever we are constrained to lift the hatchet against any tribe, we will never lay it down till that tribe is exterminated, or driven beyond the Mississippi.... [I]n war, they will kill some of us; we shall destroy them all." President Andrew Jackson reflected the prejudicial attitudes of the day: "They have neither the intelligence, the industry, the moral habits, nor the desire of improvement which are essential to any favorable change in their condition. Established in the midst of another and a superior race, and without appreciating the causes of their inferiority or seeking to control them, they must necessarily yield to the force of their circumstances or ere long disappear."[48]

The United States established its seat of power in Washington, DC. Many Americans revere Congress as one of the most sacred places in the United States.[49] Americans fancy themselves as having created a nearly perfect nation. They will sometimes admit that their democratic system was influenced by the Iroquois Confederacy. However, it is obvious that the Founding Fathers never understood the spiritual foundations that gave rise to the system represented by the Great Tree of Peace, as that formula was arrived at through prayer and ceremony more so than by political wrangling.

The newcomers never had a sacred relationship to land. It was clear from their first arrival that the land represented mainly an economic opportunity. American immigrants have long rallied around the idea of the "American dream"—the freedom to exploit the land and to enjoy its wealth. It was like a windfall—a totally free gift of land. The Vatican reassured everyone that settlement had the approval of God, and every Christian denomination since has repeated that message. In reality, it is the seemingly unlimited material resources that have made America great. But why should a people who thrust aside the hand of friendship offered by the original people of the land, and instead exploited the land to exhaustion as efficiently as possible, be considered great?

Americans take great pride in their "taming" of the "wilderness of America," which they saw as inadequately utilized by Indigenous Peoples. This windfall of untold natural riches enabled America to become the wealthiest nation in a very short time. Such "progress" was due to extensive cultivation and mining of the land, as well as the expanding use of petroleum, a cheap and powerful source of energy. Thousands of other inventions, such as electricity, the telegraph, and the locomotive, fuelled a dynamic economy. However, such a wonderland of comfort and convenience comes at a price. By the end of the twentieth century, signs were emerging that resources are not limitless and that the dream of equality for all was not being realized. The downturn in prosperity began to create dissatisfaction as the party was ending for the newcomers, whose raison d'être was the promise of wealth and opportunity. It should not come as a surprise that a people who simply saw the land as a resource to be exploited would eventually end up becoming disillusioned. The easy part was exploiting the land. The difficult part—learning to live in harmony with the environment and one another—is yet to come.

Mythologies abound in the history of the United States of America. The first myth is that God condoned the discovery and dispossession of the New World. This idea was perpetuated by the Vatican, which legally sanctioned the exploration of the Americas with the doctrine of *terra nullius*. The original inhabitants were supposedly not intelligent or moral enough to properly utilize the land, and therefore it was legally justified to usurp those territories. If Indigenous Peoples resisted, it was acceptable to fight and vanquish them—something that proved to be quite easy following devastating epidemics and the employment of deadly offensive weaponry never before witnessed in the Americas.

A second myth is that Aboriginal Peoples were barbarous and needed to be saved by a superior civilization. The wisdom of Indigenous philosophies that mandated stewardship over nature went unrecognized. Based on the myth that Indigenous Peoples were unintelligent, untrustworthy, and uncivilized savages, the colonizers believed the Aboriginal inhabitants had little to offer the settlers—nothing, of course, other than the natural riches of the land that they had carefully safeguarded for future generations: pristine forests and meadows filled with abundant wildlife and fowl and waters filled with fish that were to be passed on to their children and all future generations to come. The adage that "the only good Indian is a dead Indian" was emblematic of how Indigenous Peoples were viewed simply as obstacles to the American dream of untold riches ready for the taking. After rapid displacement of the original population, cultivation, timber cutting, and mining quickly became the order of the day. Some families were able to amass unimaginable wealth. Ordinary people gained well-paying jobs, private property, and many other benefits of a vast and naturally beautiful land. Americans felt they were truly blessed:

Manifest Destiny, was the 19th-century idea that the Judeo-Christian God mandated the immigrant Anglo-Saxon "race" to create the United

States, connect it from one coast to the other, advocate for its democratic and capitalist values, and sow liberty and the freedoms carried by assertions of natural rights to all those who would claim its birthright.[50]

These mythologies are built into the American Constitution, including the idea that all citizens will be equal and that all will be able to enjoy freedom and prosperity. It is fair to ask, freedom from what? Virtually all Europeans who came to the Americas were escaping religious or political persecution, wars, disease, or poverty. Why did they believe that they would be free of these when essentially the same fundamental political, religious, and economic systems were simply being transplanted to a new land? Freedom is an interesting concept in the sense that there is never an absolute freedom from responsibilities and structures, regardless of where one lives. Indigenous Peoples had extremely strict limits on certain behaviours, all of which were based upon a spiritually inspired set of responsibilities. In modern nations, legitimate behaviour is defined by legislated laws. Yet there appears to be an attitude among some Americans that there is no real obligation to respect the environment, let alone those who originally lived there.

As for the pursuit of happiness, this is defined largely in terms of the American dream—the unfettered pursuit of wealth and the right to enjoy it without interference. Such beliefs and attitudes run contrary to values that fulfilled the original inhabitants. It is interesting to note that Indigenous Peoples did not always seek out the most comfortable places with nice weather, such as beaches. They saw life as necessarily involving challenges and sacrifices. Their reward was for future generations to live in healthy environments.

The supposedly enlightened approaches taken by the Founding Fathers were defective in many ways. The overarching philosophy and rationale of preserving natural life was lost on them. Their primary concern was that a dictatorial government could threaten their prosperity, as the British had before the American Revolution. But the right of militias to bear arms, which may have made sense in the newly minted United States, has become an excuse for the individual to purchase deadly military-grade weapons. Similarly, the right to free speech becomes dangerous when words are used dishonestly and become weapons of mass deception in a divided society.

America is somehow divinely ordained to be the shining example to the world—that its values of democracy, entrepreneurship, and ingenuity are invaluable contributions to world betterment. While some of this potential appeared possible in the early idealistic years of the nation, once the shine comes off of American prosperity, its citizens become more disillusioned and divided. Problems of racism, inequality, substance abuse, criminality, environmental abuse, mental illness, and violence increasingly surface. Fifty quasi-independent feuding states, a president chosen by the states rather than the majority, a politicized Supreme Court, a paralyzed Congress, citizens drowning in mythology and lacking a true understanding of the origins of their nation—all of these seem like a recipe for an increasingly disunited union.

Mythologies are powerful and can be used for both healthy and unhealthy purposes. In the case of the United States, its delusions can be a danger to its citizens and to the international community. The American dream was much different from the Indigenous vision of the original inhabitants. The descendants of those colonists who came to the New World need to wake up to the reality of their exploitation and degradation of the land. There is a need to rethink what it means to live in the "New World." Is it possible to stop seeing the land as simply something to exploit, and rather to treat it as a home that needs to be respected and carefully nurtured for many generations yet to come?

Canada, while making positive advances in recognition of Aboriginal rights and self-government, is a neoliberal democracy that has made accommodations and avoided the worst excesses of its southern neighbour. But bringing about radical change is almost politically impossible, and most meaningful advances have generally come after court battles. The Truth and Reconciliation Commission's Calls to Action, which emerged out of soul-searching about the legacy of Indian residential schools, hold some promise but are still a limited guidepost. Canada has not fully recognized the United Nations Declaration on the Rights of Indigenous Peoples (UNDRIP), which calls for full recognition of Indigenous self-government and fair sharing of resources. Ultimately, the recognition not just of Indigenous rights, but of the moral and spiritual correctness of Indigenous ways is still very far off and won't happen until there is awareness and momentum to support Indigenous Peoples nationally and internationally.

RUINING THE AMAZON

Indigenous Peoples have inhabited the Amazon for at least thirty-five thousand years. Recent discoveries reveal that as many as five million inhabitants lived in extensive networks of settlements connected by grand roadways throughout the rainforest. The original soil quality of the Amazon was too poor to sustain the lushness that now exists. Scientists discovered that the abundance of today's rainforest turns out to be the result of intentional human intervention. Aboriginal Peoples discovered how to create enriched soil called *terra preta*—a mixture of charcoal and biological materials such as bones from fish, birds, and turtles. Tens of thousands of square miles of forest were covered with *terra preta* to depths of as much as six feet. In addition to improving the soil, the people introduced a variety of plants that, working together, created a robust ecosystem. Finally, the inhabitants did not exploit the environment to exhaustion, instead communally moving their settlements to new locations every five or ten years.[51]

Disappointingly, Brazil's former president, Jair Bolsonaro, who labelled Indigenous Peoples as cavemen, continued to behave like the Spanish and Portuguese conquistadores who came and destroyed Indigenous societies five hundred years ago. Indigenous leaders, led by Raoni Metuktire, submitted a case to the International Criminal Court in the Hague calling for action against Bolsonaro for crimes against Indigenous Peoples and their traditional rainforest homelands. Over 1,000 Indigenous people in Brazil have been murdered by encroaching land speculators, squatters, loggers, and cattle ranchers. All of these are a result of Bolsanaro's policies to open up the Amazon to economic development and to make Indigenous inhabitants "human beings just like us."[52] Ana Valeria Araujo, a lawyer who has defended Indigenous Peoples for over thirty years, notes: "He comes from the school that believes Indigenous peoples aren't peoples. He sees them as obstacles to development and where there's an obstacle, you have to remove it."[53]

Up to twenty thousand square kilometres of valuable rainforest, about the size of Israel, has been illegally burned and deforested annually. International figures, including Pope Francis, believe that the global community must intervene. The International Criminal Court, however, has not committed to investigating environmental destruction as a crime. If they do, it would constitute a new category called "ecocide." Brazil defends its actions on the basis of national sovereignty; however, an international lawyer observes, "The right to sovereignty cannot be equated with the right to freely dispose of the lands of Indigenous peoples, much less to have the right of life or death over them."[54] Raoni Metuktire vows to continue the struggle: "We have been fighting every day for hundreds of years to ensure our existence and today our fight for rights is global. The solutions for this sick world come from Indigenous people and we will never remain silent in the face of the violence we are suffering."[55]

The Vatican, which held legal authority over Christian monarchies, was initially responsible for creating this malaise in the Americas when it issued the 1493 papal bull *Inter Caetera*, which legitimized the claiming of lands occupied by nonbelievers. This process was not complicated—it simply involved planting a cross when landing upon the shore. There was no necessity to investigate the extent of the land, its occupants, or their traditions. Had the Vatican not intervened, things would have turned out much differently. Lacking legitimation, explorers would have been compelled to meet with the local inhabitants and establish relationships that respected their protocols. Taking such an approach, the new arrivals would have found Indigenous Peoples to be hospitable and open to establishing positive relationships. More importantly, the Indigenous inhabitants could have taught the newcomers respectful ways of dealing with one another and the environment that were different from what the Europeans were often fleeing.

WAS CIVILIZATION INEVITABLE?

Some argue that *ecolizations*, as they became more complex, would have invariably gone down the same road as European societies. However, I contend that if such societies had continued to maintain an active commitment to their spirituality, and did not succumb to materialism, modern life would not have ended up in today's degraded and vulnerable condition. In stating this, it has to be repeated that spirituality is not the same thing as religion or theocracy. Those living in ancient societies maintained direct connection to the supernal, and placed that above temporal interests. All of these relationships, especially with spirit, had to be constantly tended and nourished. To say that civilization is inevitable is tantamount to concluding that humans are inherently avaricious and aggressive and that it is impossible to create a society without greed and a lust for power over others. Such a narrative is exacerbated by myths such as that of original sin and by theories that humans are no more than genetic aberrations. Those increasingly rare surviving Indigenous communities demonstrate that it is possible to take another path.

Evidence of the success of *ecolizations* was their ability to build great monuments and settlements, as in Mesoamerica, while retaining their spiritual connections to their environment. It was the less obvious cultural and social achievements, which resulted in stable, largely harmonious, and nonacquisitive cultures, that tend to go unrecognized. The vibrancy of First Nations' belief systems and heritage has been eroded through historical contact with Europeans. Entire generations have been tragically severed from their spiritual heritage through racism, colonization, slavery, and residential schools. Unity can barely be maintained within communities that have disintegrated and become divided over the pressures of power and money.

A COMING RECKONING?

Indigenous Elders have been warning of a coming reckoning. Could it be an apocalypse akin to the biblical narrative of Armageddon that takes the shapes of devastating war, famine, economic breakdown, or crippling pandemics? A critical common threat today is climate change. There is a great likelihood that it won't be stopped, and the further threats to all life from runaway technology and artificial intelligence cannot be underestimated. They may bring an end to civilization, if not human existence itself.

The reason why humans decided to "rise up against and conquer nature" is said to have been based upon fear and the loss of trust that the Creator would provide all essentials that were needed. Remember, there was a time, not that long ago, when people remained in intimate balance with nature; when boundaries, economic development, and wars were not the driving forces of societies. Once certain groups of humans realized the advantage and power that the accumulation and hoarding of wealth gave, this led to encroachment on and exploitation and domination of other groups. Original Indigenous laws, such as humility, respect, and sharing, were thrown on the garbage heap of history. As victims of colonization, Indigenous Peoples are among the most dispossessed, experience the most intractable problems, and have the fewest resources to advance and express their way of life. But, finally, the "people without history" are beginning to have a voice and to explain their story.[56]

As a final question, one may ask why the Indigenous world, and its supposed strength based upon its spirituality, succumbed so rapidly in the face of civilization. Perhaps it was because *ecolizations* were not prepared to cope with a mentality in which physical wealth and power can be used in a destructive manner. Because Indigenous spirituality was a subtle power used to keep humanity in a healthy relationship with the world, Aboriginal Peoples could not anticipate how the colonizers would ruthlessly wield their power like a cudgel to accrue wealth and power. This kind of behaviour is unimaginable in a healthy Indigenous *ecolization* as Indigenous Elders and mentors would refuse to even entertain that type of thinking. With their world destroyed, and the guardrails of their spiritual heritage devalued, their lives would go into catastrophic free fall.

As a result of world events, it has become assumed that civilization is superior to the Indigenous societies that it displaced. However, will a closer look at ancient ways reveal that contemporary ideology is both short-sighted and ill advised?

FOUR

KNOWLEDGE AND WISDOM

WHAT WE ARE TAUGHT

s there a difference between knowledge and wisdom? Having spent over sixty years as either a student or teacher, I have come to appreciate the difference between contemporary education and Indigenous traditional learning. As mentioned earlier, the priority when instructing Indigenous youth was to ingrain a sense of one's identity as a sacred being. It was believed to be vital that copious amounts of energy be invested in teaching proper values and behaviour, in addition to practical skills. This sense of awareness of purpose and reason for being laid the foundation for a meaningful, harmonious, and abundant life.

Today, the first thing that children are exposed to learn is the alphabet, which leads to reading, and numbers, which lead to mathematics and algebra. It is true that social skills are also evaluated, and for those in denominational schools there is religious instruction. But fundamentally, is not the primary purpose for the contemporary education system to prepare youth for a life of work and generally surviving in a secular world based upon economic self-sufficiency?

In Indigenous education, children had little exposure to mathematics, let alone writing, but their societies survived well without these. For that matter, their societies also survived without monetary currencies. But what they were exposed to, apart from general survival skills, were stories of creation and relationships with animals, plants, and other beings, and to understanding their place in it all. Such stories recounted invisible spirits of nature and messages from the heavens and ancestors. These created a sense of wonderment and awe in children. But more than that, they fostered a sense of respect and connectedness, not only to the physical world but also to the transcendent. The latter became the greatest influence on people's behaviour. Other powerful tools in the Indigenous educator's arsenal were ceremony, song, and dance. In powwows, one always sees tiny children gleefully and enthusiastically imitating their adult role models. The sound of the drum created excitement, and participating in dance was an exhilarating experience of existential oneness. What better way to give youth a sense of connection to their people and to the world?

KNOWLEDGE VERSUS WISDOM

In university, the major emphasis is on intellectualism. What I referred to as "universities of civilization" in *Loss of Indigenous Eden* produce a type of knowledge that becomes a necessity when humans position themselves as being in control over everything. This means the need to fully understand how everything works to the "nth degree," hence the explosion of modern fields of science such as physics, biology, and chemistry. To be clear, nature does not require humanity's guidance in order to thrive. Indigenous Peoples had trust in the Creator and were aware that things would function very well under its divine plan. It was not necessary to have the extensive scientific and invasive technological knowledge that exists today. This does not mean that Indigenous Peoples were incapable of or uninterested in obtaining such knowledge. They were developing early science and technology. However, it is critical to understand that such developments were pursued only after being screened through the sieve of spiritual wisdom. It was never developed for purely pecuniary motives or curiosity. There had to be a divinely sanctioned rationale. For example, the many edible vegetables were produced through the guidance of ceremony, which would then lead to physical experimentation. Astronomy and architecture are other fields where the guiding hand of spirituality was obvious. Indigenous Peoples, given tens of thousands of years of careful development guided by higher virtues, would have eventually discovered all of today's sciences and technologies, and even more. However, these would have been acquired in a wisely considered way, and as such, would be safe and beneficial for future generations. They would nurture rather than exploit and destroy the environment. For example, nuclear technology initially began as research driven by curiosity, but it ended up being developed as the ultimate weapon of destruction. The threats of war have driven the development of many other technologies, including canned foods, computers, microwave ovens, jets, radar, and satellites. Indigenous Peoples never thought it wise or necessary to produce such inventions, other than for self-defence, to which all were entitled.

Today people often use words in contradictory ways. According to Indigenous values, honesty was not only highly valued but was also considered a spiritual imperative. The Creator knows if one does not tell the truth. Telling mistruths bore real consequences at a transcendent level, and such repercussions were greatly feared. Orally spoken words were taken seriously, so there was little need for writing. Truthful words were essential to preserving social trust and cohesion. Today words are too often used to confuse and divide; for example, the "fake news" that has become emblematic of our current post-truth era.

Ethics is an interesting word for moral behaviour based upon rationalist philosophy. Such guidance can be from religious texts, philosophers, legal statutes, or behavioural psychology. However, the guidance is not based on a supposition of spirituality that includes the precepts of a real and active incorporeal world and the resultant sense of responsibility for all created things. Despite the denigration by scholars of civilization, Indigenous Peoples did have concepts of law and propriety. Their belief system effectively maintained the world in pristine condition.

The term "knowledge" needs to be reconsidered in a similar manner. In retrospect, my book *The Knowledge Seeker* could have been more appropriately titled as "The Wisdom Seeker," since spiritual knowledge really is better described as wisdom. A typical definition of wisdom is "the soundness of an action or decision with regard to the application of experience, knowledge, and good judgment."[57] However, this definition has a shortcoming in that it leaves out the numinous as a vital factor in making wise decisions. The simple fact is that only knowledge that is obtained in a spiritual manner is wisdom. Wisdom explores the deeper meaning and consequences of actions.

INDIGENOUS THINKING

Art Napoleon, a scholar, television personality, and oskapewis (cere-monial helper to Elders) who is fluent in Cree, is in the unique posi-tion to interpret his people's spiritual philosophy. In his master's thesis, "Key Terms and Concepts for Exploring Nîhiyaw Tâpisinowin, the Cree Worldview," Napoleon describes the differences and challenges of speaking and thinking in Cree versus English:

> When speaking English I am not used to having to describe every single detail about a subject because this is generally not done in nîhiyawîwin [Cree] speech. After all, people are supposed to follow the innuendos, implied meanings and general tone and intent of speech. People are supposed to read body language, facial expres-sions and be able to use a variety of senses. When people are in synch, they fill in the blanks and empty spaces or just leave them for another day.[58]

Napoleon's comments suggest that outsiders may perceive that Indigenous thought is not organized or rational. Learning in the main-stream school system is based upon abstract concepts, individualism, compartmentalization, and fragmented views and information to which it can be difficult for the Indigenous student to adapt. In mod-ern education, success is granted to those who have the resources and motivation, as well as the opportunity, to master complex and linear information. That knowledge gives the individual capabilities not available to others, and gives them access to jobs, status, and opportu-nities. In Indigenous societies, necessary knowledge was available to all. Moreover, thinking occurred within an overall framework of respectful reflection. Napoleon notes that Cree learning requires speakers to think about animals, trees, and rocks as living beings and to always be aware of spirits, and to see the entire world in an interconnected way.[59]

Cree philosophy rejects notions of separation, secularity, exploitation, and attitudes of superiority, as all human life is interdependent. Those steeped in nehiyaw ways of knowing "are often intuitive, relying on dreams, body language, facial expressions, tone of voice, attitudes, emotions, mannerisms, personas and other verbal and non-verbal cues and energies. ... Cree language relies on metaphor, multiple layers of implied meanings, and how much overlap there is in between the meanings of values and laws."[60]

In other words, Indigenous communication has a versatility and ambiguity that can produce rich insight. People are able to interpret what is said according to their own interest and level of comprehension. This does not present difficulty when people are in fundamental harmony, and when exactness is not an essential ingredient in order to function within society. In English, a high degree of precision is necessary in a world where one regularly interacts with strangers who demand accurate information. In Cree, ambiguity is okay and it often becomes the subject of great conversation and laughter as one drills down into the deeper meanings of the conversation, like peeling back the layers of an onion.

Indigenous thinking is more like quantum mechanics than rational thinking because it leaves the door open and is willing to explore a range of possibilities rather than following a single prescribed path of thought. One reason is that Cree is predominately verb-based:

While English and French complexity is found at the sentence level, Cree complexity is rather found at the level of the word. In Cree, a single verb can always make up a whole sentence. This can be seen in the Cree dictionary definitions: the translations of all verbs are complete sentences. English uses many separate words and few grammatical prefixes and suffixes that combine with verbs and, to a lesser extent, with nouns. Whereas a simple English sentence might consist of, say, five or six words, the same information may be conveyed in Cree using just one or two words. In the Cree language, verbs predominate because Cree was more concerned about actions than with material objects. Of 18,000 Cree words listed, 14,000 are verbs.[61]

Cree word meanings can vary according to context. The Cree words for secular and spiritual knowledge are very close and their exact meaning will depend on context. For example, "kesig," the word for sky, in a spiritual discussion would signify heaven. Similarly, the word for star, "achak," would signify the soul. Conversations about spirituality did not occur spontaneously, but had to be engaged in subject to appropriate ceremonial protocols. Finally, there are common mistranslations. The more accurate translation for Kise-Manitow is "Benevolent Spirit" rather than "Great Spirit," as the Creator was a generous benefactor, rather than an authoritarian force acting above and dictating aspects of creation. Unlike the Christian God, Kise-Manitow was never portrayed as being in human form.

GOD OR CREATOR?

No one really seems certain about the origin of the word "God." Some say that the root possibly comes from ritualistic words for "pouring" or "summoning." Others claim it might be related to the German word for "good."[62] But a few things seem clear. Various concepts of God are unique to different cultures and the nature of this being can vary. Some religions, such as Buddhism, do not have an actual concept of God, instead referring to the presence of various harmonious or conflicting forces. In Hinduism, Brahman presides over a considerable number of lesser deities. In the Abrahamic traditions, God has a special and exclusive relationship with humanity in which humans are elevated to the central focus of creation. The concept of "God" is acknowledged by religious scholars to be a human creation. Moreover, the practices associated with religion are mediated by mere mortals in the form of rabbis, priests, or imams. Adherents are discouraged from spontaneous expressions of spirituality that fall outside of what is officially sanctioned.

There are qualitative differences between the Indigenous concept of the Creator and the later concepts of God associated with civilization. In our Cree/Saulteaux tradition, creation is perceived principally as a feminine force, in contrast to the Abrahamic God who is portrayed as male, as in Christianity. Because of their ability to give birth to life, females are seen as channelling creative power. Kise-Manitow's instructions were for people to be humble and thankful for experiencing the gifts of life and to be stewards nurturing life forms to flourish at their best. The Creator believed in unity and harmony among all groups, and did not favour any one people over another. Manitow would not grant humanity dominion over flora and fauna, nor encourage followers to destroy those observing different versions of Indigenous belief. Finally, the Creator was benevolent, not threatening.

DECLINE OF TRUTH

The technologies we have created for communication are presenting serious challenges for the transmission of truth. In his book *Amused to Death*, Neil Postman observes, "The telegraph introduced a kind of public conversation whose form had startling characteristics: Its language was the language of headlines—sensational, fragmented, impersonal. News took the form of slogans, to be noted with excitement, to be forgotten with dispatch." Photography, which means "writing with light," resulted in "the fierce assault on language made by forms of mechanically reproduced imagery that spread unchecked throughout American culture—photographs, prints, posters, drawings, advertisements...devoid of any relationship to your past or future plans."[63]

It is no accident that the Age of Reason was synonymous with the growth of print culture, first in Europe and then in America. The spread of typography kindled the hope that the world and its manifold mysteries could be interpreted, predicted, and ultimately controlled. Television and social media such as Facebook and Twitter have today become dominant influences on the formation of the public's intellectual and cultural perceptions. These media, with their broad reach and emotive power, have the ability to undermine thoughtful and considered discourse. Such media promote incoherence and triviality, and their most influential voice is one of distraction and entertainment. For a generation of children, television and social media are their most accessible companions and teachers.[64] We are now utterly dependent on the computer as essential technology. Our children will fail in school or be left behind in life if they are not "computer literate." We cannot run our businesses, or even our daily lives, unless we employ a computer. But, as humans, are we spiritually and psychologically mature enough to handle the toxicity of communication endlessly generated by such media?

According to Postman, the content of much of our public discourse has become "dangerous nonsense." Social media has redefined the dynamics of public discourse. Media technology offers viewers a vast menu of programming requiring minimal skill of comprehension. Social media is more attractive and effective as a platform for enter- tainment and gratification than for education or reflection. Thinking skills and understanding are undermined by media that require only short attention spans. Rather than educate or explain, these media gravitate towards attacks.[65]

People talk to one another less and do not exchange ideas or argue propositions as much. Glitz and glamour, and the wealth used to cre- ate it, are what are used to persuade. Postman observes that in political debates,

> the men were less concerned with giving arguments than with giv- ing off impressions, which is what television does best. Post-debate commentary largely avoided any evaluation of the candidates' ideas, since there were none to evaluate. Instead, the debates were con- ceived as boxing matches, the relevant question being, Who ko'd whom? The answer was determined by the "style" of the men—how they looked, fixed their gaze, smiled, and delivered one-liners.[66]

He goes on to lament the commercialization of media: "An Amer- ican who has reached the age of forty will have seen well over one million television commercials in his or her lifetime, and has close to another million to go before the first Social Security check arrives."[67] The result of all of this, he concludes, is that Americans are likely the least well-informed people in the Western world.[68]

Disinformation can simply be misleading information—misplaced, irrelevant, fragmented, or superficial data that creates the illusion of knowing something but which in fact leads one further from the truth. A society that can no longer distinguish truth from fiction is in real danger of disunity and conflict. Postman comments, "When a population becomes distracted by trivia, when cultural life is redefined as a perpetual round of entertainments, when serious public conversation becomes a form of baby-talk, when, in short, a people become an audience and their public business a vaudeville act, then a nation finds itself at risk; culture-death is a clear possibility."[69]

CIVILIZATION'S MENTAL BOX

Civilization is generally portrayed in glowing terms as humanity's greatest achievement. Archaeological investigations chart every twist and turn of its development from the first seeds sown to the earliest animals domesticated. There is awe at the development of metallurgy, particularly as it contributes to the ability to produce weapons that dominate others. The building of increasingly elaborate housing structures gives way to massive fortifications. The increase in wars stimulates the creation of organized militaries. Soon the Greeks and Romans are venturing out to subdue the less powerful and confiscate their lands and resources. Throughout all of this history is an amazement at, and glorification of, the ambition of conquerors such as Alexander the Great and Julius Caesar. Philosophers tout the power and wealth of civilization as historians bestow accolades of bravery and virtue upon them.

It goes without saying that the story of "progress" is one-sided. History is said to begin only when humans decide to assert their cleverness and command over their surroundings. The practices of Indigenous Peoples who survived and thrived for hundreds of thousands of years are totally disregarded and devalued. Essentially, they are ignored because they are not understood or respected. Lost are the notions that humanity can live in harmony with nature without having to control and exploit it. Indigenous stories from around the globe about coming from the stars and being allowed to experience physical life on Earth are dismissed as fantasy. Instead, a new narrative is inserted, recounting how life is a product of a biological soup and that humans are merely simians who have become superintelligent through some quirk of genetics. Indigenous protocols and practices—the idea that humans should be humble and grateful for being allowed to experience the gift of creation—are dismissed as a waste of time. The commons of nature that provided food and medicinal resources available to all is destroyed in favour of privatization, individualism, and competitiveness. Boundaries that have cut up the earth only recently are a symbol of how civilization has completely changed the face of the Indigenous world.

Because non-Indigenous academics insist on labelling prehistoric Indigenous societies as civilizations, I have had to create the counterbalancing word *ecolization*, a term suggestive of greater holism and of inclusion of and respect for the natural world. Painting Indigenous societies as budding civilizations suggests that all of humanity would have eventually gone the way of Europe—acting in self-interest, exploiting and fighting for resources, and seeing violence and greed as inherent in human character. This approach neatly discredits Indigenous ways while at the same time justifying the actions of the imperialists and colonizers. The fact is that humanity could have taken a different route by rejecting the options of selfishness, greed, and violence. The world would have been a far wiser, more peaceful, and more harmonious place.

Current society has allowed wetiko, the evil spirit of greed, to run freely. Our people greatly feared its appearance, and fought valiantly against it, by trying to heal, exiling, or if necessary killing those infected by it. Our people knew that once this spirit was unrestrained, it would be extremely dangerous, rupturing relationships and ultimately destroying the people and environments that it came into contact with. European colonizers did not realize that they had already been infected by wetiko, ever since Adam and Eve ate from the tree of knowledge of good and evil.[70] They brought it with them to Indigenous Eden, a legacy we live with to this day.

Civilization is very much a mental box in which we have all become trapped, blinding us from seeing the broader and wiser picture. Despite its allure of short-term prosperity and apparent order (enforced by coercive institutions of law), this way of life actually impoverishes and eventually destroys us. It brings struggle, suffering, and disappointment because it is unspiritual and unwise and lacks long-term sustainable strategies.

ESCAPING THE BOX

The intense devotion of academics and teachers to the idea that nothing consequential occurred in human existence until civilization arose has created an ideological and intellectual desert of our own making. Indigenous people do not view the events that occurred prior to civilization as irrelevant or meaningless. Their contemporary descendants, Indigenous Peoples today, note that the events of their existence have not been accessible to mainstream society because their significant events and achievements were not accorded the status of knowledge and achievement. Indigenous Peoples remembered their oral stories that related the ongoing flourishing and self-healing natural world. Some Elders have commented that "white people" have committed so many sins, and that so few of these have been healed, that they must be constantly recorded. History, while interesting as an account, does not impart the same wisdom that Indigenous stories imparted. Aboriginal accounts may seem simplistic, and contradictions may even arise, but what is important to note is that living the sacred Indigenous experience was taken seriously. Scholars have failed to bridge these conflicting views, confirming the dictum that humanity does not learn from its past mistakes.

In the civilizational thinking box, one is led to believe that listening to our teachers and studying all of the textbooks will solve the world's problems. Clearly this has not worked and will not work, as the basic values of civilization continue to generate the same adverse outcomes. The same principle applies to virtually every area of knowledge being researched and published by scholars. In the realm of science, untold millions of dollars are contributed to research institutions for the purpose of finding new technologies or medicines. Proponents of this approach believe that increasing the already vast array of scientific and technical knowledge will somehow bring humanity to the point of finally overcoming our challenges. The Indigenous paradigm of including spiritual protocol and inquiry as a factor is never taken into consideration.

Indigenous Peoples did have scientific capabilities. They observed their environments very astutely and were able to make impressive advances in areas such as food production. In the example of corn, the plant was identified with a spirit being. That being was revered and interacted with in a respectful way through ceremonies. It was through this sacred interaction with that plant spirit that information about its usefulness as a healing entity was gleaned. To propose controlling and harvesting that plant for profit only would be an unimaginable betrayal of our stewardship responsibilities.

Having advanced degrees with years of study, scientists will have opinions about how to solve the world's problems, such as climate change. They may advocate artificial manipulation of the weather or utilization of computer-driven technology. However, such expertise is rarely understood by the general populace. It is rare that ordinary people can question the wisdom of such specialists. From an Indigenous perspective, our knowledges were widely shared and subject to common scrutiny. But most of all, they were rooted in sacred values and wisdom. The major considerations were whether such actions were necessary and how they might affect both the natural world as well as present and future generations. Indigenous experts were generally found in the fields of ceremonies, healing, or storytelling. They were respected for their personal values, in particular their adherence to the laws of behaviour and abilities to enact them, for example by exhibiting humility and generosity. This achievement was like the equivalent of a doctoral degree.

The administration of Indigenous skills merged seamlessly with the modest needs of society and enhanced the collective ability to deal with problems. They knew how to survive on natural resources, and to resolve internal or external social problems. There is a lot to be said for keeping life simple. Today we revel in the complex economic and technological superstructures we have built. However, the sad fact is that our spiritual wisdom, to which Indigenous Peoples had paid such careful attention, was neglected and has shrivelled. Thus, these modern and technological systems turn around and damage us by creating shortages, competition, and conflict. We fail to find consensus on how these problems can be dealt with—or whether they can even be dealt with. Today's society is overwhelmed with information, but wisdom is scarce. Ultimately, in Indigenous societies the attainment of spiritual insight was a higher priority and more valued than intellectual achievement. However, this gave the appearance to outsiders that Indigenous people were intellectually lazy and uncurious. This, of course, was not accurate. It was more important that intellectualism not be allowed to escape the scrutiny of spirituality.

Having looked more closely at the shortcomings of civilizational thinking, it is necessary to examine more closely the distinction between natural and artificial and its implications for the way that humanity survives.

FIVE

NATURAL VERSUS ARTIFICIAL

GIFT OF NATURE

I n our modern world, the line between natural and artificial has become greatly blurred. It can be argued that over the course of recent human development, we have created artificial environments that provide ever-increasing comfort and convenience for ourselves, but at the expense of nature. Or perhaps we have altogether forgotten the value and importance of nature. Our penchant for creating human spaces that overlap and replace nature is a phenomenon that is traceable back to notions of human primacy.

Nature is the authentic base of life as provided by the Creator, and many see being in tune with the natural as being closer to spirituality. Aboriginal interaction with nature is intuitive, whereas society and economics are largely rational and artificial, aided by boundaries, finances, corporations, and technology. All of the latter have flourished only over the past few centuries, a period that unsurprisingly corresponds with the carving up and gutting of the Indigenous world.

Nature is a truer guidepost for survival than are human-made laws and institutions. The natural world provided Indigenous people a model to emulate. The dedication with which animals, such as wolves, raised their young was emulated. Human relationships extended to animals, who we refer to as spiritual relatives in our ceremonies. The idea of wantonly exploiting animals as commodities was not part of Indigenous ways. Although animals hunt and kill for survival, with their insights and ability to influence the environment humans are capable of transcending those behaviours. It is fair to say that in *ecolizations*, where animals were respected, the animals also respected humans. An example is the existence of a relationship of mutual respect between the dwellers of the Kalahari and lions, to the point where mutual understanding and respect existed.[71] While non-Indigenous peoples view nature as wild, unpredictable, out of control, and threatening, Indigenous people see nature as a sacred place, like an omnipresent cathedral.

Indigenous people are sometimes criticized as being hypocritical for living in modern society and taking advantage of all of its technologies. However, we, like everyone else, have the right to survival. Our Indigenous values are not easy to maintain in the hostile surroundings of secularism and materialism.

NATURE AS NURTURE

Indigenous Eden was a nurturing place. In return for the gift of experiencing life, humans were simply required to care for the Creator's gifts. Because humans are dependent on everything else to survive, it was incumbent on people to ensure that plants and animals would not only survive but also flourish. As part of this sacred relationship, our people thanked the flora and fauna whenever they were used as medicine or food.

The power of the feminine as a source of fertility was revered. Elders believe that females are specially gifted by Kise-Manitow to bring forth life and are special as life-givers. Elder Noel Starblanket told me that this is in contrast to the roles of males as hunters and defenders, which can be described as life-takers. This is why women played prominent roles as guardians of the law, as controllers of property, and in selecting leadership. Noel said that men recognized and admired female qualities and aspired to emulate those qualities. It can be concluded that the ethos of Indigenous Eden was feminine and nurturing.[72]

Predictions of how civilization might end up include as a nihilistic anarchy or as a computer-run technocracy where humans surrender our powers of intelligence and agency. There is a saying that one wants "smart guys" because they have a lot of education and know their way around the world. But for all of this smartness, why is it so difficult to address challenges as basic and obvious as climate change? Even to rationalists, it should seem irrational not to address climate and environmental destruction. The point is that we can think as hard as we can, but we won't solve the problem, the reason being that we lack wisdom. We think we can effectively assume control over nature, but really what we need is simple respect for the spirituality associated with nature. To the rational mind this process seems pointless and therefore not worth taking seriously. But Indigenous Peoples understood that the ways used to create a relationship with nature made it possible to maintain a pristine environment.

CREATING WEALTH

Indigenous economies of the New World thrived without the use of banks and currency, and they were largely self-sufficient. Barter was accompanied by formal rituals to promote good relations. Exchange of goods was based upon real value, and wealth redistribution was encouraged. The first records were simply to keep track of distributions. For example, the Inca knot system was effective for the needs of their complex society. Their use of gold and silver was not for currency but rather for the creation of sacred objects.

So what is the role of money? Money is a shared fiction, according to Jacob Goldstein, author of *Money: The True Story of a Made-Up Thing*. Currency emerged in Greek city-states in order to keep track of barter in a growing population. They began to stamp gold and silver lumps, which became the first coins and represented amounts of value owed.[73] The Chinese created coins around the same time as the Greeks. They were made of bronze with a hole in the centre to make it easier to string together and carry. The Chinese later invented paper records to track transactions. Lighter paper was even more portable and convenient. These money-based transactions enabled China's trade, economy, and population to grow rapidly. By the time of Marco Polo's visit in the 1200s, China was the wealthiest economy in the world. But back then the primary purpose of money was still more for convenience than for profit.[74]

In England in the 1600s, goldsmiths began to lend money on the promise of repayment with interest. They also discovered that one could lend more money than the value of gold in their possession. This was, in effect, the artificial creation of new wealth. The search for valuables, such as precious metals or spices from faraway Indigenous lands, further fuelled demands for financing. As competition from other European traders heated up, English investors rallied to newly created international corporations such as the Hudson's Bay Company, the British East Asia Company, and the Dutch East India Company.

By the 1700s, the Bank of England was created as a financial entity, and in France the introduction of paper money made access to credit easier, leading to an economic boom. Business was providing ordinary people with more prosperity that they could have ever envisioned. On the other hand, it was extracting a toll on the natural environment, as well as causing dramatic social changes:

> In the 1700s, life everywhere on Earth still looked more like ancient Babylon than the modern world. People still travelled the same way—by foot, by horse, by sailing ship. Most people were still subsistence farmers, usually living in some kind of hut, trying to grow enough food to not starve to death. Then, around 1800, everything changed. When you look at history, it's like there are two different economic universes: the universe before 1800 and what came after. This is the moment of the Industrial Revolution.[75]

Goldstein describes the rapid changes that came about due to economic progress, using the example of night lighting. In Babylon, a day's work could purchase enough sesame oil to light a lamp for ten minutes. When whale oil became a source for lighting oil lamps in the 1700s, with a day's labour one could light a lamp for an hour.[76] In 1850 it was discovered how to extract kerosene from oil, a fuel that was cleaner, brighter, and cheaper than ever before. But by the 1870s, inventor Thomas Edison was discovering how electricity could produce light in a bulb. His Electric Light Company, later known as General Electric, produced light bulbs, along with the first electrical power grids. Suddenly, a day's labour could produce twenty thousand times the lighting than had been possible just two hundred years earlier![77]

ERASING THE COMMONS

While Britain was becoming a leader in colonization of Indigenous lands, at home industrialization was creating an economic and cultural revolution called the "great transformation." It was a sweeping change that saw Britain transform its lands from the commons, where access to wild animals, forests, and herbs was available to all, to a system where land was legally carved up among private owners, beginning in the eleventh century with Royal Forests being set aside for hunting by the monarchy and aristocracy. In fact, prior to civilization, access to the commons was the standard way by which people accessed resources around the world. People all had the right to equally access the bounty of the land, as long as it was done respectfully. Britain pioneered the developments that would soon eventually become the norm for private property and ownership of resources that prevails today.

Surprisingly, the total growth of human societies on Earth increased little during the first 99 percent of human history.[78] The "great transformation" of the British economy and the privatization of the commons undermined people's traditional ability to lead communal lives. In the new system, they became consumers of marketed goods and individuals were forced to commodify their own labour. Wage labour and money became associated with masculinity as males were the primary breadwinners. At the same time, females were expected to be subservient and self-sacrificing consumers. Overseas, Indigenous inhabitants became another means of securing an even cheaper source of labour.

Such a setup gave a revolutionary boost to the world market system of acquisition, profit-making, and colonization. It was a destructive way to relate to lands and resources, one diametrically opposite to the manner in which generations of Indigenous Peoples had lived. Aboriginal Peoples became another cog in the wheels of the market economy, as the benefits—jobs as bankers, traders, land administrators, and government officials, and immense wealth—accrued to civilization's proponents.

ARTIFICIAL ECONOMY

Banks are a classic example of artificiality. One dollar can be taken and its value inflated twenty times through lending. This type of model is particularly apt for an economic system geared to rapid growth and resource exploitation. Banks as we know them now were originally created to support burgeoning international trade during the colonial period. Their financing made possible incredible leaps in transportation, communications, manufacturing, and colonization, as wealth increasingly migrated into the hands of political and economic elites.

Although they are ubiquitous and seemingly indispensable, banks are actually only a few centuries old. They made it possible to facilitate rapid and orderly exploitation of colonized Indigenous lands. The primary beneficiaries were not Indigenous Peoples, but rather investors, who in turn plowed money back into the development of even more employment, cultural institutions, education, and research. It is no surprise that civilization's world population quadrupled over the ensuing two centuries.

The value of money is fickle, depending on who gets to define its worth. This depends on whether bankers, politicians, and people in general have confidence in their economy. So there is a great incentive to create the appearance of financial strength. According to Goldstein, the U.S. Federal Reserve creates trillions of dollars out of thin air. The Federal Reserve realized that a nation could simply print more money and ship it off to banks when cash reserves became low. What better way to ensure rapid success and efficiency in exploiting the virgin and "free" riches of the New World? As the years have passed, financial wizards have become increasingly clever at finding ways to earn "new money," such as through money markets, hedge funds, the packaging of commodities such as questionable mortgages, and now cryptocurrencies.

In the United States, successive administrations simply ran up the national debt, which has now rocketed past thirty trillion dollars. Will there be an end to this constantly ballooning artificial economy? The abundance of resources such as oil, timber, and minerals is not infinite. Will overpopulation and increasing social decay overburden society's abilities to cope with its problems? And is a realignment of the world order also coming? It is anticipated that China will overtake the United States as the world's largest economy by 2026. Many countries will gravitate towards the Chinese yuan rather than the U.S. dollar as the world standard. Many may well view China as the more stable country, given recent political division in the United States which is laying bare the shortcomings of its societal evolution.

VIRTUAL MONEY

The latest frontier in creating wealth out of thin air is cryptocurrencies. The original motivation for creating cryptocurrency was to evade the tracking of cash, circumventing taxation by governments, as well as to avoid fallout from the devaluation of official currencies.[79]

However, in order to create trust in the system everyone is connected by peer-to-peer information that enables all users to police the system. Supporters argued that a digital system would reduce robberies of physical cash. But like any system, people learn how to scam it, and some have run away with billions of stolen digital funds with the push of a button.

Once it caught the public's attention and became a craze, the amount of computer hardware and the effort and energy to maintain the system became an obvious problem. Bitcoin miners could earn the currency by helping to maintain and manage the computer infrastructure. To reduce their immense electricity bills, such miners have moved operations to countries with low energy costs, such as Iceland, Mongolia, and China. In some cases, they use nearly half of the countries' electrical capacity, as in Kazakhstan where digital miners nearly crippled the power system. As cryptocurrency proliferates, it will consume more and more power resources simply to maintain itself.[80]

Governments are now questioning whether Bitcoin is really a currency or just a speculative investment, or even a Ponzi scheme. With its wild swings, digital currency does not have the consistency of value of normal money. Its value can swing wildly in a single day. Early users have been greatly enriched, but in the long run, especially as government regulators fail to scrutinize the system, many will see their assets evaporate into the digital ether.[81]

RETHINKING ECONOMICS

So, what does the future hold? We have seen how the production of coins, paper money, banks, and investment tools has enabled humanity to inflate economic prosperity to unimaginable heights. Indigenous peoples, who valued and respected the natural world, did not view the environment as a source of economic wealth-building. In the pre-contact Americas, they did not require currency because there was no agenda of rapid exploitation and expansion. Instead, Original Peoples took their role as stewards seriously. They were nurturers rather than diminishers of natural life. The result was pristine continents where the resources of forests, animals, fish, and birds remained largely untouched. They thrived and flourished as sustenance for future generations. But for the coming Europeans it was an irresistible feast of riches ripe for the taking.

Indigenous Peoples were not opposed to development or the creation of settlements, or to technology, science, etc. However, these were only permissible once sacred standards and protocols were met and those developments sanctioned. But all we need today is ambition and bank financing. This has resulted in rampant growth that has become a danger to nature and to ourselves. Science and rationalism have not provided the answers because they are not guided by wisdom, which would have produced safe and stable growth.[82]

Today, academics, theologians, and political leaders muse about a coming apocalypse, whether that be by nuclear war, climate change, epidemics, or other causes. Unfortunately, for Indigenous Peoples, their universe, Indigenous Eden, which was based upon respect for nature and access to common resources, has already witnessed its apocalypse. There are no state governments today that operate on an Indigenous model of governance. Spirituality has been replaced by secularism and consumerism. Sharing the commons has been replaced by real estate, bank accounts, borders, and wealthy enclaves. The overall impact of the apocalypse is obvious: where wildlife once abounded in great numbers in Indigenous lands, many species are now at risk

of extinction. Where peaceful, albeit not always perfect, social relationships existed, wars on regional or international scales are common.
Indigenous people talked about creating the best world possible for
future generations, rather than debating how soon our world might
end. Human existence was talked about in reverential tones rather
than listening to entrepreneurs brag about earning billions and send-
ing spaceships to populate the universe.

BALANCED POPULATION

Population growth is another feature of contemporary artificial life.
This is a particularly intractable policy issue that governments take
great pains to avoid addressing. There are two main theories about
optimum world population. One is that numbers should be determined by what the world's natural environment can support without
being adversely affected. According to that model, the ideal world
population is between 1.5 and 2 billion people. The last time that level
existed was in the early 1800s, just as the Enlightenment, the industrial
age, the expansion of world transportation systems, and colonization
were gaining traction. It was also the point at which the world's population of colonizers and settlers overtook that of Indigenous Peoples.[83]

The second theory of optimum world population is that it should be
as much as the system will bear. In other words, if an artificially maintained economy can be created and sustain ten billion people, then that
is fine. Countries currently encourage population growth and immi-
gration in the theory that such developments are good for prosperity.
It is also useful to have lots of bodies capable of fighting in the event a
country gets into a war. The optimal number is probably somewhere
in between the two models. If urban centres and technologies can be

developed in a way that guarantees that nature is not overwhelmed, then it would be feasible to sustain a greater-than-minimum population.

Modern mass production and consumption have grown by leaps and bounds since the 1820s, the last time when population was considered to be in balance with the natural world. This expansion has accelerated over recent decades, resulting in the human population nearly tripling from 2.5 billion in the 1950s to 8 billion today. Global economic growth is the sacred mantra of world governments. It is held out as the source of all well-being. The consumer-driven market economy in many ways is the glue that keeps modern life ticking. But in reality, this model is barely a century old. Even at a modest growth rate of 2 percent, however, the size of the world economy doubles every twenty years.

There inevitably have to be limits. Widespread and rampant use of fossil fuels has made stark the reality of carbon-dioxide-driven climate change. As human economic activity and urbanization grows, there is a corresponding crushing of the natural world. For example, it is reported that nearly 70 percent of the overall numbers of wild animals has disappeared since 1970.[84] We are witnessing diminishing and fire-ravished dying forests, plastic-polluted waters, and choking air pollution. Epidemics are becoming an increasing threat as humans come into greater contact with pathogenic viruses that are speedily dispersed via rapid international transportation.

The model that Indigenous people followed was population being in balance with the natural world. They interfered minimally with nature, and if in danger of overwhelming it, would move their settlement to a new location. It was deemed wise policy to ensure that natural populations thrived. This was the result of spiritual thinking that promoted gratitude, respect, and healing rather than exploitation. This is also why *ecolizations* had the ability to be long-lasting. Civilizations boast about empires reigning over their territories for hundreds of years. But there is every reason to conclude that Indigenous societies prospered for tens of thousands of years. This was because of simple practices of nurturing the natural world, as well as promotion of harmonious and healing relationships.

PITFALLS OF ARTIFICIAL INTELLIGENCE

Artificial intelligence is another example of an unspiritual and therefore unwise technology. Relinquishing our responsibilities to computers absolves us of our sacred mission to learn appropriate relationships. As well, these technologies further exacerbate the exploitation of resources. Last, but not least, they contribute to inequality as the owners of the technologies, whether it be Microsoft or Facebook or Twitter, increasingly amass wealth and influence. Today, technology needs to slow down and people need to demonstrate stewardship by re-evaluating the damage being done to the environment.

Automation provides a level of convenience and ease never before possible in human history. Automation has crept up slowly, from counting machines, to word processors, to quantum computers. Now there are computerized elements in automobiles and everyday items. This initial level of artificial intelligence (AI) is pretty basic, as it operates only according to how it is programmed. Someone writes a code of instructions and the systems will follow what was planned, barring some technological glitch. However, researchers want AI to go much further than simply following preprogrammed instructions:

The technology is fascinating. The advances are real. The problems seem remote. The pursuit can be profitable, and maybe wildly so.

For the most part the researchers I've spoken with had deep personal revelations at a young age about what they wanted to spend their lives doing, and that was to build brains, robots, or intelligent computers. As leaders in their fields they are thrilled to now have the opportunity and funds to pursue their dreams, and at some of the most respected universities and corporations in the world.[85]

Such developers imagine that artificial intelligence can and should be made to mimic human intelligence. They believe that such creations could benefit humanity by replacing people, who are prone to cognitive or emotional limitations, with artificial intelligences that will not only be precise and unemotional but will also have access to enormous stores of information. Part of the assumption made by such designers is that the artificial superintelligence (ASI) can be programmed to be "friendly," or at least not to be harmful, to humans. This type of AI would have information stores and processing speeds that will boggle our minds because it is so vastly superior to and more efficient than a human brain.

Apart from questions of morality, such as whether such systems would be used for military purposes, there are concerns about just how responsible and controllable such inventions will be. How can a program duplicate empathy or benevolence? Those who raise such questions admit that AI will never be human itself, but argue that with adequate instructions, such behaviours will become ingrained. However, the next logical step in the development of AI is far more controversial and perilous. This next progression will be to enable the artificial superintelligence to "think for itself." Such a step becomes dangerous as the complexities of the AI system become even too complicated for its human creators to comprehend. The idea is that, given the amount of information and rapidity of decision-making, ASI could conceivably not only fix itself but also improve its own performance.

James Barrat, author of *Our Final Invention,* agrees that a point will be reached when the artificial intelligence systems and technologies will become so complex that no single person, or even any group, will be able to understand and manage all of its complexities. Will artificial intelligence simply take over and direct all of human activity? If ASI controls complex infrastructure necessary for society to survive, these could theoretically be shut down for unknown reasons and without any effective intervention on the part of technicians.

This will be a sad and sorry state for the future of humanity. Barrat believes that by this stage humans will no longer be in control. Is it possible that the ASI will eventually make decisions that favour its own welfare as opposed to that of humans? Barrat fears so:

> Without extremely careful programming, a superintelligence might discover that it's confined to a "sandbox," a.k.a. a virtual world, and then attempt to escape. Once again, researchers would have to access their ability to keep a superintelligence contained. But if they managed to create friendly AGI (artificial general intelligence) it might actually prefer a virtual home to a world in which it may not be welcome. ... It may not take long for a creature a thousand times more intelligent than the most intelligent human to figure out it is in a box. From the point of view of a self-aware, self-improving system, that would be a "horrifying" realization. Because the virtual world it inhabited could be switched off, it would be highly vulnerable to not achieving its goals. It could not protect itself, nor could it gather genuine resources. It would try to safely leave the virtual world as quickly as possible.[86]

In other words, it would not allow humans to stand in the way. Barratt concludes, "Maybe researchers will wake up in time and learn to control AGI.... I believe we will have horrendous accidents, and should count ourselves fortunate if we as a species survive them, chastened and reformed. Psychologically and commercially, the stage is set for disaster."[87]

Fortunately, such artificial superintelligence is still not quite there. But plenty of warnings are already being issued about the serious disruptions that ChatGPT and deepfakes can cause society. From an Indigenous perspective, one must ask, Why go down this road? Has any computer programmer engaged in genuine spiritual ceremony and prayed to consider the wisdom of such technology given the Creator's purpose for humankind? If they had, these young, "bright" technical wizards would have thought differently.

UPENDING CLIMATE

According to the United Nations Intergovernmental Panel on Climate Change, without action our current trajectory will see the earth warmed up by four degrees Celsius over preindustrial levels by the year 2100. Parts of "Hothouse Earth" will definitely be uninhabitable due to heat, desertification, and flooding. It is estimated that there will be hundreds of millions of climate refugees by the year 2050. Southern Europe and northern Africa will be in permanent drought, and deserts in the United States and China will greatly expand. With sea levels rising by nearly ten feet, many major cities and significant parts of countries, including Bangladesh, India, and the United States, will be under water.[88]

Seventy percent of Earth's surface is covered by water. The oceans currently play an extremely significant role in mitigating the effects of climate warming, absorbing 90 percent of the excess heat. However, by absorbing so much carbon, the ocean gradually becomes acidified. This change has disastrous effects on organisms that are sensitive to acidity, such as crustaceans and those in coral reefs. It is estimated that by 2030, 90 percent of coral reefs, which support the most varied life in the oceans, will die. Finally, in absorbing extra heat, ocean waters become warmer and less able to absorb oxygen—dealing another blow to sea life.[89]

It is possible that in the long term, feedback loops, such as methane leakage from melting permafrost and the release of heat stored in oceans that are reaching their capacity to absorb heat, will cause global heating to spiral to unimaginable levels. In a world that is eight degrees warmer, oceans will rise by forty feet as ice caps melt, inundating two-thirds of the world's largest cities. Temperatures would be so oppressive that, in the desert and in the tropics, humans will not be able to move freely in the daytime lest they perish of heat exhaustion, where the body dehydrates, leading to organ failure and heart attack.

In a warming Earth, forests will be steadily consumed by raging fires all around the globe, from Brazil to Central Africa, Indonesia, and northern Canada and Russia. In Canada, the 2023 forest fire season, only halfway through at the time of this writing, has been record-breaking. There have been 3,400 fires, far more than average, that have burned twenty-eight million acres—about the size of the state of Virginia; 155,000 people have been forced to evacuate their homes. For the first time, Americans have felt the tangible effects, with hazardous smoke affecting much of their northeast, including New York, Chicago, and Washington, DC. The force of hurricanes and cyclones will cause damage of epic proportions. Land and sea species will perish in the thousands, and with them much of the food base people rely on, in what has been dubbed the "Great Nutrient Collapse."[90] Climate chaos will see nations fight over diminishing resources. Refugees will flee sub-Saharan Africa, South Asia, and South America in the millions.[91] Humans will experience immense displacement and suffering, but with clever abilities to adapt, a few may survive. However, will people want to continue to bring children into such a dysfunctional and hostile world?

The effects of climate change will whittle away at economic production so that by 2100, 25 percent of the world's vaunted prosperity, so prized by governments, will be wiped out. Yet today the United States continues to subsidize the fossil fuel industry to the tune of five trillion dollars per year.[92] We are mesmerized by the illusion of current progress. David Wallace-Wells, author of *The Uninhabitable Earth*, writes about human pride, arrogance, and wilful blindness:

Those who have imbibed several centuries of Western triumphalism tend to see the story of human civilization as the inevitable conquest of the earth, rather than a saga of an insecure culture, like mold, growing haphazardly and unsurely upon it. That fragility, which pervades now everything humans might do on this planet, is the great existential insight of global warming, but it is only beginning to shake our triumphalism.[93]

Repeated stories of widespread destruction cause mental stress on individuals, including anxiety and depression, particularly among youth as they witness the impotence of governments. Politicians tend to bury their heads in the sand, refusing to acknowledge that such drastic changes could occur so quickly. It is characteristic of the rational mind not to believe something until it is seen. The problem is that by that point the damage is done and it is too late. These are the costs of civilization that accompany the belief that God made humankind all-knowing and all-powerful, and that the creation of our artificial human world at the expense of nature was okay. We have not abandoned our hypnotized fixation on progress, endless economic expansion, and population growth. Why are we so impotent in the face of existential threat?

What are some of the changes to our way of life that will be required to turn things around? Will it be possible to decarbonize the economy without extreme loss of jobs and industries? Admittedly, the world's infrastructure will require major rebuilding. But even green solutions such as electric vehicles will present other types of harm that may be just as damaging to the environment. Perhaps the real answers are those we don't want to consider—a smaller population that is more in line with the earth's natural carrying capacity, or the winding down of the banking and financial systems that enable the artificial lifestyle that we perceive as our lifeblood. It will require major resolve and courage to bring about these changes.

Should the Indigenous worldview influence how people think? David Wallace-Wells thinks so:

We are still, now, in much of the world, shorter, sicker, and dying younger than our hunter-gatherer forebears, who were also, by the way, much better custodians of the planet on which we all live. And they watched over it for much longer—nearly all of those 200,000 years. That epic era once derided as "prehistory" accounts for 95% of human history. For nearly all of that time, humans traversed the planet but left no meaningful mark. Which makes the history of mark-making—the entire history of civilization, the entire history of what we know as history—look less like an inevitable crescendo than like an anomaly, or blip. And it makes industrialization and economic growth, the two forces that really gave the modern world the hurtling sensation of material progress, a blip inside a blip. A blip inside a blip that has brought us to the brink of a never-ending climate catastrophe.[94]

Wallace-Wells suggests that humanity needs some sort of spiritual awakening that will bring humanity back to caring for the earth and acting with stewardship, in essence what Indigenous spirituality has a always taught.

Humanity possesses unique gifts of reflection and the ability to manipulate its environment. Of these gifts, the most unique and valuable tool is our intellect. Next, the dangers of using the mind without wise guidance will be examined.

SIX

DANGEROUS MINDS

QUESTIONING OUR PLACE

hilosophy, which originates from the Greek word *philosophia*, "love of wisdom," is a pursuit of questions regarding issues such as the nature of existence, the nature of mind, and morals. In particular, metaphysics examines the nature of reality and epistemology looks at the nature of knowledge. Socrates (470–399 BCE) claimed he did not necessarily possess knowledge but was principally a pursuer of wisdom. But central to him and his successors, Plato (424–347 BCE) and Aristotle (384–322 BCE), was the role of humanity itself and how people could achieve fulfillment.[95] Plato was a great proponent of the use of reason as opposed to "superstition" or "supernatural thinking." Aristotle carried this insight further by emphasizing that the common person has to use their own judgment in order to distinguish between good and evil.

While Greek philosophers maintained that plants and animals had a sort of "soul," humans, by virtue of their intellect, were positioned well above the rest of creation. This idea of the separation of humanity from the rest of created beings was the beginning of the departure from countless millennia of Indigenous belief. From the latter's perspective, being reliant upon and interdependent with nature meant that humanity and nature needed to coexist rather than be separate.

Humanity's increasing preoccupation with its self-image and ability to dominate nature is a pattern that progresses from Egyptian to Greek and Roman cultures. The departure from Indigenous values also manifested itself in religious form. Religious figures going back to Abraham (around 2000 BCE) declared that humans are the central focus of creation. Greek abandonment of humility was a further step towards eating of the fruit of the tree of knowledge of good and evil.

Abraham is an enigmatic figure. No one knows for sure where or if he even existed, as no archaeological evidence has been found. He is renowned as the first monotheist and the founder of the Abrahamic religions—Judaism, Christianity, and Islam. Everything that is known about him is what is contained in the Bible. Different traditions have Abraham doing various things, including being a nomad, a preacher, and a scholar. It is written that he lived 175 years, and that along the way he fathered children in old age.[96] The essential story of Abraham is his faithfulness to God in the face of multiple challenges such as plagues, disease, and deaths. Abraham's obedience is tested when God instructs him to kill his son Isaac, something he is prepared to carry out until stopped at the very last moment.

Bruce Feiler, author of *Abraham: A Journey to the Heart of Three Faiths*, suggests that part of the legacy of Abraham is to be prepared to kill in the name of God.[97] But the most significant aspect of Abraham's story is his condemnation of what he considers to be the idolatrous worship of nature gods.[98] The verdict of biblical scholars is that Abraham should not be considered to be a historical person. Rather, he should be seen as a mythological figure that represents an emerging way of seeing humankind's place in the world.[99] The process of civilization had been unfolding already as individuals began to cultivate crops and domesticate animals. The prophet simply gave the emergence of civilization and its human-centred focus the stamp of divine sanction.

As centuries of "civilization" unfolded, European thinkers increasingly glorified human culture, wealth, military conquest, and territorial aggrandizement. Correspondingly Indigenous Peoples were portrayed as uninformed, undisciplined, weak, and therefore inferior. This choice, by what was initially a small group, unleashed the belief that humans could control and manipulate the world for their own purposes. This siren call of material prosperity created the illusion that the more humanity achieved, the more it was competent to secure its own long-term survival. That attitude became humanity's greatest vulnerability.

DISRESPECTING OTHERS

Early Greeks perceived disturbing differences between themselves and barbarians. Unknown peoples were portrayed in myths as beasts and subhuman creatures.[100] Greek philosophy and culture aimed to bring order out of chaos, at least from the perspective of their values. They could not trust nature, but rather had to bring it under their own hands. Barbarians were seen as obstacles to the Greeks' pursuing their idealized civilization and enabling it to spread. In the process of creating the world's first empire, Alexander the Great's conquest of the "savages" extended as far east as India. He then imposed Greek culture on the vanquished.[101]

As noted earlier, the Greek attitude of superiority was epitomized in Aristotle's theory of natural slavery, which justified enslavement of the uncivilized because they were perceived as inferior. Slaves played an essential role in creating the prosperity of the Greeks' widely heralded democracy, but they were not accorded the rights of citizenship. The Romans adopted the same approach when it came to their treatment of Indigenous Europeans: "As tallied by Plutarch, Caesar's armies killed one million barbarian enemies of Rome, enslaved another million or so along the way, subjugated some three hundred-odd tribes of savages, and destroyed eight hundred of their towns and cities during his seven-year-long campaign."[102] Aristotle's theory continued to be the moral basis for slavery during the European colonial period in Africa and the Americas.[103] Similar thinking influenced Americans' reasoning about their destiny and the justification for subjugating "inferior" Native Americans. Writing about the Indigenous Peoples of North America, Thomas Jefferson observed,

Occupying a country which left them no desire but to be undisturbed, the stream of overflowing population from other regions directed itself on these shores; without power to divert or habits to contend against it, they have been overwhelmed by the current or driven before it; now reduced within limits too narrow for the hunter's state, humanity enjoins us to teach them agriculture and the domestic arts; to encourage them to that industry which alone can enable them to maintain their place in existence and to prepare them in time for that state of society which to bodily comforts adds the improvement of mind and morals.[104]

RISE OF RATIONALISM

The European Renaissance, which took place between the fourteenth and seventeenth centuries, was focused on the philosophy of humanism and the glorification of the arts and literature. Accompanying this exultation of humanity's image and accomplishments was the Age of Reason. The elite were giddy about how quickly fascinating scientific discoveries in astronomy, mathematics, geography, physics, and physiology were being made. They convinced themselves that through "progress," which came only through our wit and ingenuity, humanity could solve every problem to build an increasingly perfect world.

Philosopher and scientist Rene Descartes's famous line "I think, therefore I am" further positioned intellect above all else.[105] But a fundamental disadvantage of rationalism was overlooked—that thought thrives in a world of dualism and relativism. In rationalist thinking, each side of an intellectual debate inevitably finds an argument to negate the other. Anything that can be advocated in rational argument can also be contradicted. There is no absolute or transcendent authority to act as an ultimate arbiter and unifier, so there is always a winner and a loser.

OUR SACRED RESPONSIBILITIES

Humans are gifted with unprecedented intellect and selfawareness. However, thought that does not recognize a spiritual purpose for life and responsibility for respecting creation is lacking. Intellect without sacred grounding is a dangerous and damaging force. The intellect is considered by our people to be one of four aspects of being, the others being physical, emotional, and spiritual. Of the four elements, spirit is considered to be the most fundamental, as it is the place of our origin as well as the home to which we eventually return.

Rationalists portray Indigenous allusions to spirit as fanciful portrayals of reality. For example, they will say the "White Buffalo," which represents the sacred, is nothing more than a genetic mutation. However, the real point is not about the mutation but about what stands behind that symbol. It was more important to remember the meaning behind events than the specific details. Others claim that Aboriginal Peoples were slow to develop science because of their "superstitions." However, Indigenous people are perfectly capable of observation and analysis and made advances in many areas such as agriculture, astronomy, and architecture. The difference was that they were reluctant to manipulate nature if it was deemed spiritually unwise or if there was no pressing need.

Rationality cannot adequately address climate and environmental destruction because it does not act until these phenomena are finally established in studies and analysis. Scientists are doing little more than documenting the demise of the planet without giving clear insight as to how our attitudes and lifestyle will need to fundamentally change. Indigenous wisdom advocates preventative action to nip the problem in the bud before it festers. We can intellectualize as much as we want, but the problems of degradation will not be solved as long as there is meagre regard for spiritual oversight.

Once humans purport to assume control over nature and all other aspects of life, we find ourselves needing to develop as much expertise as possible in order to manage things. However, when Indigenous Peoples kept their faith in the Creator, they did not have to study everything exhaustively. In the end, leaving matters in the hands of Manitow proved to be a better long-term strategy for survival. Human tinkering is only making things worse. In fact, the easiest way to support nature is also the simplest: not to interfere with it at all.

The Enlightenment and its knowledge systems, such as those promoted by universities—political science, economics, engineering, etc.—have been the driving influence on global development and the dominant social ethos over the past few centuries. Scientific discoveries have often been motivated by profit, as well as by the need to innovate in times of war. In terms of the span of human presence, the paradigm of secularism is extremely recent. What occurred in the Americas after contact was a huge unleashing of wetiko, the spirit of greed. Society is now dominated by materialism, avarice, social breakdown, mistruth, crime, environmental degradation, and species destruction.

CONFUSED MINDS

Mind disconnected from spirituality becomes like a boat lost in turbulent waters or, worse, like a rabid dog, out of control and dangerous. This paradox is what exacerbates the excesses and craziness of contemporary culture. People are becoming "unhinged" as a result of sensing that they do not have a purpose in life. Humans are also able to exercise free will, but that freedom can lead to either positive or negative outcomes. Mi'kmaq Elder Albert Ward warns, "The mind is different. It is different because your mind is, we could say, it is black magic. If you let your mind do all kinds of things for you, your mind takes over your body and your heart."[106]

It can be stated that non-Indigenous thought has become trapped within the civilization box. Within this box, it is believed that meaningful human history and activity did not begin until people began to exert control over nature. The entirety of their experience and relationship with nature comes to be interpreted through the lens of human self-interest. This mindset leaves Indigenous knowledge and philosophy outside of the box. Instead of seeing the period prior to civilization as one in which humans were defining their relationship with the world in terms of spirituality, humility, thankfulness, and a sense of stewardship, this period is portrayed as a one of wasteful stagnation. Instead, the liturgy of the Abrahamic traditions, Greek thought, and Roman aggressiveness are lauded as the elements that have made humanity great. The exploits of explorers, military leaders, captains of industry, scientists, and industrial magnates are held up as the ultimate role models.

Throughout history, intellectuals have waged relentless ideological warfare against Indigenous Peoples, claiming that the latter never had sophisticated philosophical, moral, or scientific systems. For simply trying to protect their people from the wealthy and powerful trying to usurp their lands and destroy their cultures, they were labelled savages and barbarians. They are painted as lacking control over their emotions, being inherently violent, and having a tribalism that promotes warfare.

Once within this mental box, those people no longer have access to Indigenous wisdom, ceremonial heritages, and harmonious social practices. An ideological system that prevailed globally for hundreds of thousands of years has been replaced, especially over the past two hundred years, by wanton abuse of resources, overpopulation, over-consumption, and social division. We have abandoned the Indigenous agenda of working to perfect and solidify spiritual values.

We have been in the post-respect era since the rise of civilization. We are in the post-generosity era with our individualism and private property. We are currently in the post-truth era, where fake news and disinformation are staple tools of politics. Where in Indigenous Eden the truth would be stronger than the sword, there is every reason to admit that in civilization the sword is actually stronger than the truth.

This is not to say that there are not individuals today who are paragons of honesty, generosity, etc. The problem is that they have to live within a social framework that increasingly rewards selfishness and dishonesty. When the mind is deprived of the oxygen of truth, humility, generosity, and wisdom, it will gradually deteriorate. Powerful individuals, adept at accumulating wealth and power, become the worst examples of success. The period in which Indigenous Eden flourished could be called the "Age of Wisdom." It has now been replaced by the "Age of Reason." Unless it can be restored, Indigenous wisdom will be lost as the guiding light for humanity.

BIASES OF ACADEMIA

Applying the word "civilization" to Indigenous cultures is a form of intellectual imperialism. It implies that all human cultures would inevitably go down the road of selfishness and greed. Such a mode of thinking essentially dismisses the ancient Indigenous philosophies, such as humility, thankfulness, sharing, sacrifice, and stewardship, and redefines the world in terms of human self-interest. As inheritors of the Enlightenment, anthropologists were not equipped to appreciate and understand the principles of ancient, let alone contemporary, Indigenous spirituality. They were trained to deny the validity of anything that could not be grasped by the mind and witnessed physically. With their rationalist bent, the focus was on parsing every minute discrepancy in Indigenous accounts. If one Indigenous group reveres one spirit and another group a different one, there is no possible consistency in beliefs, they concluded. These observers "missed the forest for the trees."

Scholars point to any transgression by Indigenous people to prove that they are "just like us." All societies make mistakes. The Aztec abandoned their virtue of bravery and became fearful and distrustful of nature when they saw convulsions such as eclipses, volcanoes, and earthquakes. As a result, they carried human sacrifice to an unhealthy extreme. Aztec Elders had warned that this practice was unhealthy and, if not curtailed, would result in their demise. The prophecy came true in the form of the arrival of Cortes, who cited the sacrifice as evidence of evil. Eventually the Aztec would have figured out how such natural processes actually work. Indigenous *ecolizations* that remained faithful to spirituality were able to eventually overcome wetiko. In another example, the Haudenosaunee, who had become embroiled in internecine violence, reformed their approach towards conflict when they created the "Great Law of Peace" that mandates that discussion must replace violence.

By interpreting the entire range of human experience starting with the lens of civilization, eons of Indigenous perspectives are erased. Had historians fully comprehended the ideology and legacy of Indigenous Peoples, it would have been determined that this new lifestyle was suspect. In order to correct this mistake, perhaps history should be renamed "ourstory" to be truly inclusive. Ourstory would then bring Aboriginal Peoples and their 97 percent of the time of human experience into the equation. It would also open up peoples' minds in a way that frees them from the mental box of civilization.

REASSESSING UNIVERSITIES

The definition of knowledge is "facts, information, and skills acquired by a person through experience or education; the theoretical or practical understanding of a subject."[107] This definition does not appear to accommodate spiritual experience, although theoretically it could. Having a relationship with the transcendent was a normal manner of obtaining knowledge in the Indigenous world. Excelling in Indigenous spirituality was similar in effort to obtaining a doctoral degree or training for the Olympics.

Universities are among the greatest proponents of civilization, touting the greatness and wonders of human achievements. They teach the arts and sciences of human domination and the exploitation of nature. Their rationalist approach deviates from Indigenous values in two ways: it obviates the need for spiritual guidance and inspiration, and it promotes "head thinking." Head thinking emphasizes categorization and differentiation, as well as valuation of superior intelligence, as opposed to heart thinking, which prioritizes the maintenance of harmonious relations.

Philosophy, which addresses issues such as the reason for existence, moral and ethical behaviour, and the quest for knowledge, is highly rationalistic. An examination of textbooks used in philosophy courses reveals virtually zero reference to spirituality. Philosophy fails to recognize that the transcendent is not only tangible but is also a higher form of intelligence. Spirituality goes beyond the concepts of ethics and morals defined by thought alone to a deeper sense of being. Philosophy needs to appreciate that respecting the numinous does not automatically mean the abandonment of reason. In fact, such wisdom enhances and edifies knowledge. Elders place high importance on the development of intellect, but realize that it can only be accomplished properly within a context of genuine reverence.

Science can be described as "the intellectual and practical activity encompassing the systematic study of the structure and behaviour of the physical and natural world through observation and experiment." The scientific method is defined as "a method of procedure that has characterized natural science since the 17th century, consisting in systematic observation, measurement, and experiment, and the formulation, testing, and modification of hypotheses."[108] The apparent success of science in manipulating the material world has given it an aura of legitimacy and invincibility.

One can master chemistry textbooks full of formulas. It appears at first glance that Indigenous knowledge has nothing to contribute. But why are so many chemicals produced that destroy the environment, not to mention poisoning people? Why are pharmaceuticals of dubious usefulness being pumped out primarily to produce profit? If Indigenous chemistry was practiced, would these types of things be allowed to occur? With a sacred protocol process guiding science, the question would be raised as to whether the investigation or the outcomes would benefit future generations. By comparison, ethics and morals have limited value, as they are governed by rationalistic rather than sacred thought.

Although the ethereal is not measurable by scientific instruments, it is a valid component of knowledge because the detrimental consequences to humanity of ignoring it are real. It is a higher form of intelligence that transcends rationality and materialism. This is why ancient knowledge systems managed to produce societies that were not only productive but also healthy and stable.

Recorded history began with Herodotus around 500 BCE, so it is a recent development in terms of our human story. Indigenous Peoples recollected their past orally in order to preserve their sense of inherent identity and place in the world. When negative occurrences happened, these were remedied through healing so that society could move forward without continually bearing scars.

The bias of historians is obvious: the only story worth telling starts when humans begin to act in their own self-interest. They fail to understand that for a far greater period people did not act like that. Yet it is not difficult to discover what the ideology of "primitive, prehistoric" peoples was. Those ideologies continue among contemporary Indigenous Peoples. Elders still maintain that our true identity is that of spirit beings experiencing a physical journey, that in return for the gift of experiencing physical life, we were to be grateful and act as stewards, and finally, that we are not the central purpose of creation.

Political science deals with partisan thought and behaviour and with systems of governance. Governments are concerned with the distribution of power and resources and analyze this in different ways depending on whether they are, for example, democracies or dictatorships. This discipline is a reflection of contemporary ways, a study of an endless struggle for power and wealth between groups, each having different priorities. The left and right wings of politics are actually not different, in the sense that they both deal with the same divisive nature of civilization. Absent is the idea that a transcendent authority can be the ultimate arbiter of human affairs. Theocracies are also different, as they position the priorities of their religion as the primary authority, with ideologies and edicts that are often hostile to Indigenous values. Finally, governments pay little attention to the rights of "non-humans" which Aboriginal Peoples consider to be their kin.

To Indigenous people, spirituality is the highest practice of politics. Indigenous protocols would greatly benefit international leaders. Imagine if world leaders had to go through the same procedures as Indigenous leaders. The meeting would preceded by four days of ceremony including fasting and cleansing sweat ceremonies intended to purify thoughts and intentions. Leaders would listen to the wisest and most highly respected Elders speak about how humans are to engender good relationships through humility, honesty, respect, love, generosity, courage, and wisdom. They would be reminded that they have sacred responsibilities. After this rigorous preparation, then the leaders would be prepared to go into discussions and ready to make the wisest decisions, not only for the present generation, but also for future ones.

Economics is another characteristic tool of civilization that needs to realize that the fundamental goal of the economy should be survival. Economics is concerned with maximizing the production, consumption, and distribution of wealth. In the Canadian context, economic activity is based upon capitalist and globalist models. Banking enables the steady expansion of economic activity. Original Peoples in the Americas did not need to employ money or banking systems that distorted the intrinsic value of goods. In other words, non-Indigenous economics were not intended to facilitate rapid exploitation, expansion, and enrichment. Market-based economies cater to human demands, but at the expense of diminishing natural life forms and resources that are the true bases of well-being. The financial system unfairly permits a very few individuals to amass incredible wealth and power at the expense of others. This system damages social relationships and carries immense potential for abuse.

Geography should realize that land is more than just real estate and a resource to exploit. It has only been a few centuries since private property and borders have carved up the commons. Earth is a macrocosm of living elements that provide the foundation for human well-being. Rather than quantifying and measuring for exploitation, the emphasis needs to be placed on recognizing the unified nature of life. Geographers need to distinguish between a natural balance with nature and that which has been created by artificial human systems. It should be demonstrated that nurturing the environment and depending on the commons for mutual benefit should be paramount.

The fine arts, particularly painting and sculpture, have historically been concerned with aesthetics and depicting beauty, usually with the intention to produce idealized human images. Art needs to distance itself from works intended only to magnify human pride and achievements. The art of traditional cultures instead portrays relational aspects of nature, particularly from a spiritual perspective. The other important role of art is for healing. Humanity does not need further self-absorption and pride. Oscar Wilde once noted: "My own experience is that the more we study Art, the less we care for Nature."[109] To sum up, based on how they teach subjects and pursue research, universities are information-rich, but wisdom-poor.

INDIGENOUS MENTAL HEALTH

Indigenous healers were the first psychologists, promoting meaning, balance, wholeness, and connectedness. Elders say that there must be an experience of spirituality in order for there to be a psychology of healing, as it goes beyond one's ego's needs. Ceremonies like smudging, pipe ceremonies, and sweat lodges all initiate intense interaction with the supernal.[110]

Western psychologists insist that psychology be controlled by certified professionals. Their obsession with measurable outcomes means that spirituality is reduced to religious data, such as attendance, attitudes, and effect on behaviours. Altered states of consciousness tend to be negatively associated with drug or alcohol abuse or psychotic states. Therapists tend to discourage exploration of altered states of consciousness. As psychology professor Dick Katz contends, "It's almost as if psychology protects itself from a serious, sensitive study of spirituality, by configuring it as an unrecognizable, even threatening monster of an experience."[111] Katz maintains that Western psychology needs to become less domineering and be open to learning from other traditions:

> Whereas Indigenous approaches to psychology go, in the course of daily living, into and within the spiritual nature of the universe, mainstream psychology keeps drawing lines of separation from that journey, insisting on its fallibility, questioning its reality. Historically, to achieve its goal of not only being a separate discipline but a respected one at that, psychology believed that it had to remove itself from its roots in religion and philosophy, in order to become a "true science," which meant a laboratory-based field of inquiry.... Mainstream psychology's primary response to spirituality is to deny or ignore, or at least minimize, the existence of spirituality as an experiential phenomenon, and, in particular, as emphasized in Indigenous approaches, spirituality as a personal experience.[112]

Indigenous teachings about the transcendent can help move mainstream psychology beyond its individualistic, ego-focused perspectives: "When these people come to our ceremonies trying to 'find themselves' and focus on the drama of the spirits that have come to them, as if it's a personal accomplishment...I worry because they seem to be missing the point. We seek spiritual guidance so we can better serve others and our communities. We pray for the well-being of others," says Elder Danny Musqua. There needs to be an exchange of intense energy to bring about profound change.[113]

Indigenous "psychotherapists" heal others not just by themselves but also with the help of community. The first step is to create a kinship relationship with the seeker, often as between a grandparent and grandchild. They may not be able to relate to the individual's specific issue, but they help them as fellow human beings who need to be brought back to a healthier state. The process involves ceremonies such as the sweat lodge, where an individual goes through symbolic cleansing and rebirth. This can bring remembrance of one's earliest conceptions of his or her life's purpose. Therapy can involve physical tools such as herbal medicines, but it can also involve delving into dreams or visions.

According to Musqua, "balance is what we seek. Balance is what allows us to be fully human. Yes, spirituality is key, but without feeding our physical, emotional, and mental lives as well, we're out of balance. We're not healthy. We're not preparing for our return to the Creator."[114] He adds, "Respect goes beyond, way beyond, respecting each other. Respect means protecting the environment and all of its creatures, and realizing that we must fit into that natural order."[115] To improve psychology there is a need for new approaches that can acknowledge, respect, and incorporate Indigenous practices. For example, along with ceremonies, talking circles can be powerfully effective. Musqua points out, "We knew and know about the unconscious…The unconscious is also the pathway through which the spirits and supernatural understandings can sometimes enter into our human world."[116]

The psychologist as researcher generally maintains power and control, leading to an imbalanced power structure and inability to allow spontaneous interaction with and feedback from clients. In the Indigenous system, participants are all equal and communication is more free-flowing. The focus on individualism in society has grown largely out of the history of settlement and colonialism. People have become pioneers without the benefit of their extended families. It became incumbent on them to act as strong individuals in order to survive. The problem, however, is that approach risks losing relationships with and responsibilities towards a community. It is too easy to pick up roots and move without much care for those left behind.

To Indigenous Peoples, relationships are key aspects not only of social and psychological well-being but also of the harmonious functioning of societies. Where there are strong relationships there exists a strong culture of maintaining responsibilities towards others. Those who are more capable, powerful, or wealthy will be sensitive towards the needs of others.

INDIGENOUS PARADIGM

Elders are our philosophers. The Old Ones have always been willing to discuss issues in a respectful and sacred manner. They spend hours debating fine points of knowledge until consensus is reached. However, they have not had the benefit of the scholarship of thousands of academics in multitudinous universities over the years through which they could voice their philosophy. This is one reason why Indigenous thought is so little understood. Elders do not outright reject all intellectual and technological advances made by the non-Indigenous. They recognize and accept that intellect is an essential feature of being human. Their concern arises when the intellectual function becomes divorced from the sacred. Placed under the microscope of spirituality, it becomes clear that much contemporary knowledge and many technological systems are unwise and need to be revised or eliminated.

Why is there is no role for the supernal in science? Some of the world's most renowned scientists are open to that idea. David Bohm, who was a protégé of Albert Einstein, theorized that consciousness is everywhere and pervasive throughout the universe, and that conservation of information and energy imply that even human consciousness can somehow supersede death. He suspected that there is an implicit order that scientists do not fully understand. This implicit or unseen system affects what manifests the world of physical reality. Einstein's insights into general relativity, the nature of matter, and so on did not come from rational analysis but rather through intuition, a process akin to Indigenous perceiving. He made reference to God in his musings and realized that discovery of the theory that enabled nuclear weapons was unwise. He acknowledged that there exists far more than meets the eye:

> The belief in the existence of basic all-embracing laws in nature also rests on a sort of faith. All the same this faith has been largely justified so far by the success of scientific research. But, on the other hand, everyone who is seriously involved in the pursuit of science becomes convinced that a spirit is manifest in the laws of the universe—a spirit vastly superior to that of man, and one in the face of which we with our modest powers must feel humble.[117]

Indigenous Peoples were capable of observing the world and finding ways to impact it. However, they had a different approach based on spirituality rather than on "hard science" characterized by clear and verifiable results of experimentation. Did they have an approach based upon their perceptions that all created things have spirit and could be related to through ceremonies? In his book *The World We Used to Live In*, renowned scholar Vine Deloria was certainly convinced, describing reliable accounts of medicine persons growing corn to full height in a matter of hours and their ability to miraculously heal gaping wounds, ability to influence weather, such as causing rain, ability to make food appear, and ability to revive recently deceased persons. There are numerous historical accounts of the ability of shamans to locate lost persons and objects great distances away. This was accomplished through the practice of out-of-body or spirit travel.[118] These phenomena were discussed in my book *The Knowledge Seeker*.

Art Napoleon notes that individuals who are inclined towards spiritual pursuits can be "recognized as having gifts that can sometimes alter the natural order: conduct healing, find lost objects, foretell the future, travel through time and space, communicate with animals and other spirits, find game, and control physical and natural elements like the weather, just to name a few abilities."[119]

It is noteworthy that scientists today recognize that they cannot grasp or understand the 95 percent of the cosmos that exists in the form of dark matter and dark energy. This milieu is almost certainly the abode of consciousness and spirit. If physical instruments are useless in such an environment, is it possible that consciousness itself can be the tool of experimentation and that more than one person having transcendent experience is the proof? Would it not be a good thing if this methodology leads to tangible results that enhance rather than degrade our relationship with the physical world?[120]

Is it possible to resolve the ideological conflict between materialism and the ethereal? Some ask how it is possible to make decisions outside of the rational framework when one consults the ethereal. What if it is proven that one can receive precise information that is not otherwise rationally accessible? I discussed such a question in my book, *Loss of Indigenous Eden*.[121]

WHITHER THE FUTURE?

The Enlightenment—the idea that human intellect could solve all of the world's problems—ushered in a flourishing of the sciences, arts, education, and technology. But in the act of rejecting anything having to do with the numinous, a wealth of wisdom was lost. This has produced our current dilemmas. We labour under the illusion that rationalism is the highest order of thought, and that the institutions it has produced will be sustainable. But can they last the next thousand years, let alone another 800,000? Essentially the Enlightenment has served our selfish, short-term vision of prosperity and happiness. It is a powerful illusion that binds our minds within narrow confines, and we are beginning to sense, but not clearly see, the dangerous trajectory humanity is following:

The richest eighty-five people in the world control more wealth than the poorest half of the planet's population. Nearly 8 million American kids suffer from mental disorders, with prescriptions for psychotropic drugs for kids up 49% just between 2000 and 2003. ... Despair darkens ever more lives as rates of clinical depression and suicide continue to climb in the developed world. A third of all American children are obese or seriously overweight, and 54 million of us are diabetic. Preschoolers represent the fastest-growing market for anti-depressants, while the rate of increase for depression among children is over 20 percent annually in recent years.[122]

Writers like Richard Dawkins confirm the verdict about our behaviour when they conclude that there is no God and that humans are inherently selfish: "Let us try to teach generosity and altruism, because we are born selfish."[123] Dawkins throws up his hands and blames it all on our genes. But that's a mistake. It's not human nature that makes us engage in the blind destruction of our world and ourselves. For hundreds of thousands of years, human beings thrived on this planet without creating such problems. This is not about the nature of our species, but rather the consequence of our choice— civilization, the structure within which our species has become trapped:

> Most of the dangers civilization claims to protect us from are, in fact, created or amplified by civilization itself.... If it's making us unhealthy, unhappy, overworked, humiliated, and frightened, what's all this progress really worth? We know more or less what it costs: nearly everything. We can tabulate the forests destroyed, topsoil eroded, fisheries depleted, aquifers fouled, the atmosphere pumped full of carbon, the cancers, the stress, the desperate refugees, and more. People used to talk about leaving a better world for their children. Now we just hope they'll somehow survive the mess.[124]

Having seen the defects and dangers of civilization and the rational mind, it will be instructive to revisit Indigenous culture and lifestyle to see how it functioned as a successful system without having to engage in quests for wealth and power.

SEVEN

CULTURE AS LIFESTYLE

VIABILITY OF INDIGENOUS CULTURE

ndigenous societies were well positioned to be sustainable over the long term. Did Indigenous *ecolizations* have the potential to survive for tens of thousands of years or more? If so, what were the cultural ingredients that made this possible? The historical attitude towards Indigenous Peoples is that they were ignorant, uncreative, unprogressive, and therefore backward. European explorers perceived Aboriginal Peoples as being lazy and unproductive. Ceremonies, which often went on for days, were regarded as wastes of time. According to these explorers, whatever spirits or gods Indigenous Peoples followed must be causing them to be dull. And with indolence, the thinking went, there must be corruption and immorality. Indigenous Peoples were not industriously tilling the soil, mining the earth, or constructing battlements. They appeared to have little achievement to show. These people had no moral system, it was believed, and therefore colonizing them would be justified, even if just to save their souls. Of course, in retrospect we know that the real motive was to exploit their lands and resources. But did the newcomers miss something?

A recent news article points out that Australian Aborigines are the world's "oldest civilization."[125] Again, we see the misuse of the word "civilization" as there is little evidence that Australian Aborigines displayed the characteristic values of civilization. As an *ecolization*, they remained humble, intimately connected to nature and to the spirit world. This is why they have been able to persist for sixty thousand years. However, after a mere few centuries of contact with Europeans, their cultures are severely damaged, as is the natural environment of animals and plants that they relied upon.

Indigenous lifestyles were sensible and effective. What Indigenous Peoples were doing was respecting their spiritual wisdom. To them it was wrong to declare that humans were the masters of nature and to dominate and control their animal and plant relatives. There was an intimate relationship with the flora and fauna. Ceremonies and protocols promoted respect and gratitude for the existence of these non-human beings. They offered thanks whenever hunting or harvesting. In doing so, these plants and animals flourished and were available whenever people needed them.

The abundance of buffalo, deer, wildfowl, and fishes when Europeans arrived in the "New World" was testament to the effectiveness of these policies and practices. Taken together, these resources of the commons met human needs, particularly when there was great care taken to ensure that human populations did not overwhelm the balance with the natural world. There were protocols for respectful access to, and sharing of, resources, which enabled groups to live harmoniously beside one another. Of course, things were not always perfect, but when conflict arose, restoring peace, healing, and harmony were top priorities.

The primary objectives of Indigenous societies were not the pursuit of economic and political power, but rather the perfection of their spiritual moral values, such as the Seven Virtues, which were in fact the prevailing laws. Violation of these norms could result in censure and even death. In such a world, day-long labour was not a necessity, although Indigenous people were perfectly capable of working hard when the need arose. This left ample time for the important work of honing spiritual values and fostering a harmonious world.

JOYS OF CULTURE

Indigenous cultural activities were not merely pastimes—they were also important social and therapeutic events. Music is considered a sacred gift of Kise-Manitow, the Creator.[126] Powwow drumming is also a spiritual activity. For drummers, the sound represents the heartbeat of Mother Earth. The steady beats of the drum lull the mind into calmness and can induce a meditative state. It induces a sense of timelessness, while at the same time reminding one of the cycles of life. This is true of Indigenous people around the world and is why the drum is the oldest instrument created. Sacred songs could be received in dreams or visions, and each song has a spirit.

Our music reflects our strength and joy in life. Singing has significant personal and social therapeutic benefits. As a form of social activity, it creates positive personal relationships. Such interactions are relaxing, and enjoyable. Singing can boost one's mood, confidence, and mental health. In fact, it is a common therapy for those with mental illness or dementia.

Music reflects people and their times. Religious music reflects the beliefs and reverent mood of previous eras. Symphonies reflect the mood of the Enlightenment and the awe and optimism of new scientific insights and advancement of the arts. Military songs are creatures of times of conflict and designed to evoke patriotism. The Pink Floyd song "Money," with its backdrop of the sound of cash registers opening and closing, is reflective of materialistic life. It is no accident that techno music was popular in manufacturing areas such as Detroit. Similar comments could be made about other genres, including baroque, country, elevator music, techno, punk, and rock music, as well as African-inspired music such as blues, jazz, soul, rap and black metal. Our traditional music showed our reverence and respect for nature—the gifts of the Creator which sustain us and which we are only asked to be stewards of. Indigenous music and its natural rhythms now compete with the music of civilization, whether it is hymns, opera, martial music, pop music, rap, or heavy metal.

The cultural practice of dancing is not only social—it is also healing. Children love movement and it creates a powerful lifelong attachment to their culture. Dancing has significant social and health benefits. According to educators, the benefits include focus, relaxation, a sense of purpose, feelings of well-being, and connection to others and inner self. The very act of collective dancing—of moving in unison and having the dance reflect cultural values or stories—is a valuable instrument of social cohesion and collective identity. Besides being enjoyable, it is a great source of exercise that staves off the aging process. It provides a form of entertainment and fulfillment that brings people to want more, and to avoid less healthy activities, such as watching television.

Indigenous people played group games such as lacrosse. However, the emphasis of such activities was more on cooperation than on competition. As a social activity, sport helps to define an individual's capabilities and status within a group. In that sense, it is an important facet for defining relationships and self-worth; for example, when it comes to abilities to hunt, trade, or act in defence of the community. One is left not only with a feeling of enjoyment but also with a sense of self-esteem and self-worth. Even sporting events can be learning environments by beginning with an opening prayer that acknowledges the gift of life and the need to respect creation, rather than with jingoistic national or team anthems used to rouse the crowd.

Something as simple as beading can also prove to be both a relaxing as well as a socially stimulating experience. It allows creativity to produce something beautiful and functional. Well-made clothing was not only a useful product, but was also a statement of the individual. Indigenous culture invested more into spiritual and cultural capital than it did in accumulating wealth and power, and these investments paid off handsomely in terms of social stability and health. It is incumbent for reconciliation that respect and honour be shown to Indigenous music and culture generally.

MEANING AND LONGEVITY

Despite dressing in garb laden with furs and feathers, Indigenous Peoples were not slaves to nature, as they were often accused of being. They are renowned for their crafts. But leather clothing and beadwork are more than decoration—they reflect an intimate connection with nature. By maintaining a respectful relationship with nature based upon steward-ship, Aboriginal Peoples avoided the worst abuses of their environment. Through their relationships with plants, Indigenous Peoples of the Americas learned techniques that enabled them to become fantastically successful agriculturalists who grew a wide variety crops. Moreover, with careful management and respectful politics, it was possible for people to have security of livelihood. Competing for resources, building massive defensive fortifications, or developing devastating weaponry was needless.

What is there not to like about an Indigenous lifestyle? People had a deep sense of spiritual purpose and self-worth. There was ample time for relaxing social activities such as drumming and dancing that created close social bonds. By sharing abundant resources, everyone felt appreciated and cared for. There was always certainty that the future would be better than today.

REFOCUSING EDUCATION

Reconciling with Indigenous wisdom will be essential to human longevity, so it is imperative that steps be taken to incorporate revised narratives in educational foundations, curriculum development, and teacher training. There also needs to be honesty about the destructiveness of civilization. An authentic curriculum on Indigenous spirituality has yet to been written. There is a need for a new metanarrative that reflects the centrality of spirituality in Indigenous thinking and teaching. Some elements could include the following:

- Indigenous origin stories that feature travelling from stars as consciousness are widespread and far older than the theory of evolution.

- Prehistoric people were Indigenous and were intelligent, not primitive. Indigenous intellectual development is focused upon spiritual wisdom.[127]
- Indigenous spirituality existed before religions and contained the "original instructions." These beliefs were more holistic, pragmatic, and universal. Guiding spiritual principles involved treating one another with respect and being stewards of creation.
- Spirit is real and has actual impacts, and Indigenous people communed with nature through ceremonies rather than worshipping it.
- Civilization has only been around for approximately 6,000 years, which is only the last 3 percent of the human experience of 200,000 years. It was an error for historians to begin the interpretation of human experience commencing with civilization.
- Historic Greeks and Romans should not be referred to as ancient but rather as part of the recent past.
- Indigenous culture is oppressed because its values are not consistent with those of civilization.
- Indigenous societies are better described as "*ecolizations*," as they were nurturing, rather than self-absorbed and violent like civilizations.

Current curriculum on Indigenous spirituality can be characterized as superficial. Most emphasis is on traditional ecological knowledge— the idea that Indigenous culture and beliefs had a close relationship with nature and that Indigenous Peoples knew the intricacies of how animals behaved and what plants could be used for medicinal purpose.

Elders are brought in to share stories and legends. What the curriculum lacks is a deeper explanation of the basics of Indigenous beliefs and how spirituality informs their thought, attitudes, and life in general. Deeper wisdom was traditionally passed on through stories and ceremonies that produced insights that are substantially different from that of mainstream education. Perhaps most importantly, these traditional approaches instilled a sense of awe, reverence, and respect for creation, rather than teaching analytical and technical skills that it is wrongly believed will enable us to control and manage the world.

SPIRITUALITY AND HEALTH

Indigenous Peoples regarded healing as an important instrument of health. Mainstream medical care focuses on repairing physical, emotional, and mental damage, but does little to address the underlying cause. Appreciating that spirituality plays a significant role is difficult for the contemporary health care system to grasp. In Indigenous tradition, there are four aspects to being: physical, emotional, intellectual, and spiritual. The sacred was able to play a central role in traditional health because people lived in an environment that is far different from our current work-oriented and resource-exploitative world.[128]

The instructions for restoring and maintaining wellness were clear. Among these was a strong belief in the existence of spirit. Humans are spirit beings having a physical experience in order to learn proper relationships.[129] Since we are not the central purpose of creation, we need to be appreciative of the gifts of creation and be stewards. Ethical behaviour includes the Seven Virtues: respect, courage, generosity, honesty, humility, love, and wisdom.[130] Finally, Indigenous Peoples placed the greatest emphasis on their spiritual life, with ceremonies emerging as the main tools. Ceremonies renew connection with spirit, and they play key roles in spiritual, emotional, and physical healing.

The Indigenous approach to health and wellness was holistic and preventative. It began with a foundation of beliefs that we are to live harmoniously with the natural world. The animals and plants could teach people healthy ways and where to find natural remedies. The traditional healer did not claim to have supernatural abilities, but instead was able to open up the healing force that each of us can access by ourselves. Such healing forces were very powerful when operating within the dynamics of Indigenous Eden. Faith in spirit forces has sometimes proven capable of bringing about healing where mainstream medicine has given up hope.

Elders do not discount the value of mainstream medical techniques. Virgin soil epidemics of previously unknown diseases such as smallpox carried away up to 90 percent of communities in one fell swoop after first contact with non-Indigenous peoples. The experience of smallpox on the prairies in the 1700s and 1800s, and the efficacy of the Hudson's Bay Company's cowpox vaccine to save lives, made such an impression that it led to the demand to include the medicine chest clause in the Numbered Treaties.[131]

Ceremonies alone cannot repair damage to kidneys or lungs caused by modern living. This is where mainstream medical knowledge is valued. Traditional healers recognize that the spiritual help they offer may not be enough to alter a health outcome. The intrinsic value of the Indigenous approach to health is largely that of guiding individuals into a healthy lifestyle that prevents the encountering of illnesses. In that sense it is holistic and preventative. It does not necessarily require highly trained medical professionals or expensive facilities and treatments. From that perspective it is a more financially sustainable approach.

Looking forward to the need for mainstream society to find a more effective method of ensuring health and wellness for all, the Indigenous model is instructive. The health system cannot be perpetually geared towards only handling crises. The COVID-19 pandemic, and future anticipated outbreaks or disasters, show how easily the health-care system can be overwhelmed. Why not take the Indigenous approach and deal with underlying issues of wellness, rather than just the approach currently being taken? Contemporary society does not deal well with spiritual beliefs, believing these to lie within the personal realm. However, Indigenous spirituality is not denominational, in the sense that it does not require belonging to a particular church, synagogue, temple, or mosque, etc. It simply requires attention to one's spiritual life, especially the strictures of humility, honesty, courage, love, generosity, respect, and wisdom, and reinforcing such observances as through ceremony.[132]

MENTAL WELLNESS

Mental illness is one of those afflictions increasingly plaguing the world. The Elders see phenomena such as anxiety, depression, and socio-pathology as spiritual illnesses. This is an area in which Indigenous wisdom is capable of playing a meaningful role.[133] In Indigenous culture, much time was spent cultivating one's spiritual responsibilities. Everything else then fell into place, including the ability to find and utilize the necessities of life, acquire social harmony, and maintain health. It was an approach that sustained the world's Indigenous Peoples well before civilization came along with its pursuits of wealth and power.

In terms of mental health, the collective belief that there is a higher purpose to life, and that help is available from Kise-Manitow

(Benevolent Creator) and supportive spirits, gave a sense of comfort. Within this framework, individuals and communities were able to develop their intellectual capacities in a healthy way. Indigenous ways prioritized the cultivation of morals, as embodied in the Seven Virtuous Laws, over intellectual development. There needed to be morally valid justification to exploit resources or to develop technologies. It was also necessary to consider whether such developments might harm our animal and plant kin, or bring negative consequences for coming generations. Above all wetiko, the spirit of greed that could destroy individuals and societies, had to be kept at bay.[134]

SPIRITUAL MATURITY

Perfecting inner moral maturity was on the top of the cultural priority list for Indigenous "*ecolizations*." They understood the dangers of ignoring principles of virtuous behaviour. The focus of traditional education was not the ABCs or 123s, but rather spiritual learning and perfection. Had Indigenous societies not been forcibly displaced, our current world and life would have been far more respectful, peaceful, and healthy. Humanity has not achieved the inherent maturity required to responsibly handle all of the power, wealth, and technology that civilization has spawned. We live and interact with technologies, many of them lethal, on a daily basis. But in our hubris, we refuse to recognize their danger or consider the need to give them up. Observers of contemporary society recognize that there needs to be a major paradigm shift and readjustment in consciousness. That paradigm is right in front of us—it is the Indigenous one that enabled humanity to survive successfully for eons. It will be a daunting task, seemingly impossible, but it must be undertaken.

Indigenous Peoples, who valued divinely inspired wisdom as a higher level of knowing, were on a path that could have enabled humanity to last one million years, as our simian relatives are expected to do. Though well rewarded with apparent prosperity, civilizations have made unwise choices that have brought humanity to its current tenuous state. The warnings of Elders that a reckoning is coming are already materializing in multiple forms: climate change, epidemics, artificial intelligence, and species extinction. Unfortunately, civilization prevents Indigenous Peoples from utilizing the powers that they know work best: humility, respect for creation, healing, and renewal.

What is the most effective path forward? Is it to find solutions by creating even more technologies and artificial intelligence? Is it inevitable that society will fall into anarchy? Or is it advisable to look at returning to Indigenous principles through rediscovering this ideology and these sensibilities as a viable way forward?

EIGHT

RETURNING TO STEWARDSHIP

EDEN'S APOCALYPSE

Upon "discovery," Indigenous lands and resources, carefully nurtured over eons, came under the control of peoples with a completely different ideology. There was no sacred relationship with the land and its flora and fauna. The primary value of the land was as a commodity to exploit and sell. Any obstacles that got in the way of these objectives, including Indigenous Peoples, would be unceremoniously swept aside. Rather than respecting the land as a birthright carefully tended to flourish for future generations, this entirely new philosophy placed maximum priority on rapid exploitation and profit. It is not a surprise that billions of passenger pigeons, shot for sport, would disappear virtually overnight. The same was nearly the case for the tens of millions of buffalo that roamed much of North America.

Should it be a surprise that, after only a few hundred years of non-Indigenous management, the air and waters are poisoned by pollution, that there is talk of the extinction of species, or that nations argue over access to resources? The discovery of the Americas was not the greatest thing to happen to humankind, but rather an unfortunate collision. A new chapter of world history opened in which civilization and all of its abuses against nature received new impetus. The apocalypse of Indigenous Eden simultaneously occurred. Annihilated was a world in which harmony with nature and respect for one another was standard wisdom. Given more centuries, Indigenous Peoples would have evolved equally complex social, economic, and technological systems, but these would have been achieved in safety and harmony with nature.

Indigenous Peoples were considered to be backward and unprogressive. However, these supposed traits were, in fact, the product of deliberate social practice. Indigenous policy was not to exploit the environment as quickly as possible, but rather to preserve natural wealth. They nurtured nature by not interfering with it and allowing it to flourish. This is how resources such as millions of buffalo and billions of passenger pigeons were abundantly available for everyone's needs. Indigenous Peoples' priority was not intellectual and material progress, but rather the attainment of spiritual development, including observance of the Seven Virtuous Laws. Elders maintain that this effort is more difficult work than what we do today because it involves self-control and sacrifice, such as in fasting and sharing.

Indigenous Peoples are not anti-intellectual or against "progress." Human development and Indigenous spirituality are not seen as mutually exclusive. However, it is modern thinking that fails to accept that spirituality is a real and overarching factor that supersedes rationality and science. It is the indispensable tool that provides wisdom about the best way for humanity to move forward. People must make profound changes in the way we think about things. This is particularly true when it comes to long-term survivability.

SUBDIVIDED WORLD

We have all grown up studying, in school, maps with boundaries between countries. It seems as if they have always existed and are a normal part of the landscape. However, they are, in fact, only a few centuries old. Most have been developed, in conjunction with the carving up of Indigenous lands, to prevent conflict between colonizers over who controlled which territories. Once in control, colonizers created boundaries that restricted access to communal resources, abandoning the Creator's original plan. Boundaries and laws became essential to manage conflicting interests. Global institutions such as banks and corporations played a major role in establishing the modern world. But are their long-term impacts actually more damaging than helpful in terms of global welfare?

One of the strictures of both Indigenous beliefs and in the Bible was that humans act as stewards of creation. However, what this means is a point of confusion. In today's world, that may be interpreted as doing ecological studies, protecting forests from overlogging, stopping the pollution of water or dumping of plastics and toxins into the oceans, or preventing animals from being hunted to extinction. These are all part of the modern mitigation approach. To Indigenous Peoples, however, there was an extremely simple solution: just allow nature to flourish without interference. Actions taken to nurture nature, as the Indigenous inhabitants of the Amazon demonstrated, helped the rainforests to thrive. The products of such policies were evident upon the Europeans' arrival on

Turtle Island. These newcomers found so many fish that they could be scooped up by the basketful, flocks of billions of passenger pigeons that literally darkened the skies for days, and in the west, the landscape was covered in brown as herds of bison moved across the terrain.

DECIMATION OF WILDLIFE

Within decades of European arrival, the wealth of those resources would collapse as passenger pigeons became extinct and the buffalo were brought to the brink. In Europe and Africa, the decline of wild animals was following a similar pattern in the face of civilization. The American Bison, whose population is estimated to have been around 60,000,000 at European contact, was reduced to fewer than 1,000 by 1900, a nearly 100 percent extinction. In Africa, elephants, estimated to number 27,000,000 in 1800, are now reduced to 400,000—a 98 percent decline.[135] Giraffes, numbering 2,700,000 in 1900, have now only 68,000 remaining—a 97 percent decline. Rhinoceroses, numbering 1,000,000 in 1900, have declined to 22,000—a 98 percent loss.[136] Lions, which once numbered 400,000 and roamed much of Europe and the Middle East but were hunted to extinction, are reduced to 20,000 in protected areas of Africa.[137] There are many other examples around the world.

It should not be a surprise that the newcomers, who had no sacred relationship with the land, would so quickly abuse it. The Indigenous Peoples who welcomed them believed that the new arrivals would understand the need to respect creation as they had been directed by Manitow. It came as a rude awakening when the newcomers claimed the land as their own, erecting fences and boundaries and marginalizing the original inhabitants as if they were simply a hindrance. The carefully maintained riches of the Indigenous Garden were rapidly expropriated and sold by auction to the most avaricious takers. The land became valued for little more than the profits that it could produce financially, creating artificial rather than natural wealth.

TAKING STEWARDSHIP SERIOUSLY

The COVID-19 pandemic and international repercussions reveal the vulnerability of the human-made global economy. The pandemic has laid bare the entire artificiality of our contemporary lifestyle. Epidemics were not widespread in prehistoric times because the conditions that supported them did not exist. Before agriculture, humans didn't live with domesticated animals from whom they could contract pathogens that could mutate into dangerous diseases. Tuberculosis, cholera, smallpox, and influenza are among the scourges that spread with the arrival of civilization. Today viruses propagate quickly due to our advanced transportation systems and overcrowded cities. Overpopulation is an intractable problem that is not being addressed. Overbuilding and extreme density are only made possible by our artificial economic infrastructure. The current model of growth, based upon capitalism and endless exploitation of virgin resources, is not sustainable and has outlived its usefulness. Greed truly is the Achilles heel of humanity.

Spiritual protocols of consultation and discussion will be essential to reform mainstream education, economics, culture, arts, entertainment, politics, technology, etc. In each of these areas we will need to apply Indigenous knowledge and protocols to gain new perspective. For example, should profit or ambition be the primary motivating factors in making long-range personal decisions? It is obvious that, as humans, we are not the originators of the world and the universe. Yet we act as though we own all of it. We alter it to our whim and dream of fantasies that we might someday populate and command the entire universe. Incredible are the heights of human self-deception and foolishness.

We believe that we have evolved biologically and that, by virtue of developing superior brains, it is through our own efforts that we have become so creative and powerful. That is a lack of humility. Our Indigenous ancestors prized humility as the most important of our spiritual laws, an insight that impeded people from making foolish or rash decisions.

The current proposed solution to fighting climate change is the development of "green technology" intended to replace oil and gas technology. However, it turns out that such green solutions stand to create almost as much environmental disruption as they are intended to prevent. The development of electronic vehicles will require mining for rare earth metals such as yttrium and europium. However, since such elements are typically found in low concentrations, a great deal of mining activity is required. Apart from direct damage done by mining, there will be the creation of mountains of toxic waste, and the accompanying dangers to the health of mine workers.[138] Solar panels contain highly toxic metals, which at present time are not adequately recycled. Hydropower causes significant disruption to water bodies, aquatic species, and waterfowl. Biomass created by stagnant water contributes further to methane emissions. Wind power appears to be less intrusive but is in fact damaging to bird species. The point is that green technology is driven by the usual motivations of civilization—money and power. Solutions that were damaging would not meet approval by Indigenous planners.

THE RECKONING

If the balance with nature cannot be restored (e.g., reversing climate change, pollution, exploitation, etc.), there will arise a real threat to human well-being. Preliminary indications are that humanity will be unable to deal with the most glaring danger it faces: climate heating. We seem oblivious to the danger of our own undoing, like lobsters in the cooking pot. Scientists predict major catastrophes and painful suffering with what is to come. It will not be an overnight catastrophe. There will be subtle impacts, such as humans simply choosing not to reproduce in the hostile world of the Anthropocene, where life support systems have severely degraded. Humanity will likely end with a whimper and the earth will hardly notice as it moves to heal itself.

Population reduction is one of the most intractable challenges facing politicians and one with which they are least inclined to deal with. Politicians are loath to compel people to have fewer children, as fewer people imply less economic activity and fewer soldiers to join defence forces. Any successful approach needs to incorporate motivations that supersede simple human self-interest, including basic respect for animals, plants, and all other natural entities. We must recognize that everything is connected and that we need to take responsibility for our selfish decisions.

There are two prevailing theories of optimal population. One can be seen as an Indigenous model: having a population that does not encroach upon, damage, and diminish the natural world that supports it. With this model, the desirable world population would be around 1.5 billion. This number was last seen in the 1820s, the point at which the non-Indigenous population overtook Indigenous numbers. In the 200 years since, world population has ballooned over five times to nearly 8 billion people.[139]

The other prevailing view of optimal population is basically "whatever the system can bear." This is a population model based upon the ability of the artificial human economy and infrastructure to support population. As long as there is land to develop, banks to finance new housing, food stores to nourish mouths, and adequate education and health services, things are well and fine. This type of growth has been promoted over the past two centuries by massive population relocation to Indigenous lands and the unfettered extraction of minerals and oil, cutting down of forests, and elimination of flora and fauna. Replacing them are economically profitable cattle, pigs, chickens, crops, factories, and cities, etc. The belief is that there is no limit to growth and things will continue to expand as long as humans benefit.

Grocery stores are a glaring illustration of the artificial food system. Where at one time everyone had access to the commons to hunt and forage, now food production has become the specialized activity of large corporations that decide prices and manage the quality and distribution of food. One can walk down the store aisle and see long arrays of cut and wrapped meat. There has been no work put in by the consumer to track down and process the kill, let alone give thanks to its spirit. One might argue that store shelves are the only way to ensure that the meat is safe. But this sidesteps the question of why meats have become disease-prone or contaminated in the first place. Human intervention and activity has created conditions that would be rarely seen in the wild, where animals lived in self-regulating healthy settings. The final insult of the artificial food chain is that much ends up being thrown away as waste. One third of all food produced in the world is lost or wasted—approximately 1.3 billion tonnes of food annually. If not for the wastage, the world's 800 million undernourished people could all be fed.[140]

DO WE CARE?

Attitudes of wastefulness are not surprising given ideologies of resource exploitation, rapid economic growth, and colonization that have created today's world. According to popular American culture, the "New World" was a gift, granted by God, in order that the United States thrive and become the greatest nation on Earth. While such myths have been useful to justify the settlement of the "New World," to Indigenous Peoples it has been an apocalypse—the total destruction of their ways of thinking and being. The "discovery" of the Americas can be viewed as perhaps the most devastating development that could have occurred for long-term human welfare. The ransacking of the Americas was a major engine of growth that emboldened the international frenzy to discover, pillage, colonize, and overthrow Indigenous cultures all over the world. Such developments exacerbated privatization, the creation of national boundaries, the proliferation of money through international banking systems, and the explosion of increasingly devastating military technologies.

How will it be possible for humanity to survive for the next 800,000 years? It is time to be realistic. The campaign to prevent a climate catastrophe is proving to be a dismal failure. Power-hungry politicians have demonstrated that they care more about pandering to voters than about providing strong and wise leadership. It is a weakness of the nature of politics. The only questions remaining are how bad can environmental conditions become and will humanity be able to adapt?

Given humankind's current downward trajectory, we have largely lost pragmatic understanding of how the power of spirituality can nurture and heal. Instead, we throw money as a solution for resolving problems, or threaten devastating wars. While we have achieved incredible insights into science and technology, our spiritual evolution and maturity has sorely lagged. We have rarely stopped to consider the employment of spiritual protocols to determine whether scientific and technological developments are wise. Instead, the siren call of profit, ego boosts for making new discoveries, or the need to develop ever more deadly weapons to keep competitors at bay have been the driving forces.

EXERCISING MORAL POWER

Governments have invested a great deal of resources in controlling the thinking of their citizens. This is most apparent in authoritarian countries. Mosôm Danny told me that the political systems he was concerned about the most were communist countries. The reason was their lack of recognition of the supernal level, with communist doctrine treating the numinous as a sort of opiate of the masses—something that is useless because it is an obstacle to paying attention to maximizing material gains. Along with the dismissal of spirituality comes "realpolitik," an "ends justify the means" mentality. Ruthless persecution of citizens is justified as long as it serves the national purpose.

The rise of the People's Republic of China is said to present the greatest challenge to the United States' global power. China has a population that is four times as great as that of the United States, and its populace is relatively homogenous. Chinese culture has developed over millennia and they have historically maintained a close connection to their land. The Chinese have long had a large population, but they historically persisted in maintaining an agrarian economy that served their needs without the need for the wholesale exploitation of resources. It is true that the Chinese experienced internal convulsions as groups vied for power. However, they never directed this power towards world conquest. It was only with the advent of European colonizers, who exploited the Chinese and caused the Opium Wars of the mid-1800s, that China was forced to adapt technologically and militarily in order to resist European domination. That modernization process has continued, with China now poised to become the world's largest economy. Admittedly, China is exhibiting characteristics of modern aggression, with military build-up in the region and expanding economic interests reaching as far as Africa and South America.

During my tour of China in 1982, I learned of internal debates as to whether Chinese "chauvinism" would be a positive or negative factor in international diplomacy. It was still a time when shop goods were left on the street without fear of being stolen and the preferred method of local city transportation was the bicycle. Granted, much of this was due to tight government control over the economy, including where one could work. Today there has been adoption of the worst of the modern world economy, including the inequality and pollution that comes along with it. I also learned about the Indigenous roots of China. Prior to the rise of Confucianism, the primary belief system of China was Taoism. It is an ancient Indigenous belief system, followed by about 15 percent of the population, that recognizes sacred connections to ancestors and harmony with all aspects of nature.[141]

Indigenous ways used "soft power," the cultivation of positive relationships instead of force, in pursuing goals. This promoted respect, caring, stewardship, and healing, which would foster greater health for existing and future populations. Indigenous "power" differed from that of civilization, which, it could be argued, disrespects the natural world and acts aggressively towards the less powerful. The United States of America, unlike China, does not connect to its Indigenous heritage, instead denying that its original population ever contributed anything of value. Despite claims of moral superiority, the United States does not hesitate to flaunt its economic and military might when useful. If China retains connection to its Indigenous heritage, and restrains chauvinistic impulses to exploit and control weaker countries, could China be more trustable as the world's leader?

Colonization produced quick and tangible "progress" in the form of lavish lifestyles, military forces that can project national might, and other necessities of surviving in a violent world. Historians revel in the exploits of the empire-builders, and their tomes suggest that the most noteworthy events in human experience begin with acquisitiveness and aggression. As for those on the receiving end of civilization—the Indigenous Peoples—their experiences, thoughts, and feelings hardly merit attention. Their lives were considered to be boring and unproductive, or as Hobbes liked to say, "nasty, brutish, and short." Of course, none of this was true, but the narrative, wielded like an ideological weapon of war, succeeded brilliantly in justifying the global rape and enslavement of Indigenous Peoples and the dispossession of their lands. This dynamic of avarice reaped great and tangible rewards for the short-term, but has the wielding of this power been wise or healthy for humanity? The verdict is becoming increasingly obvious. Indigenous "power," while not as compelling, would have created an underlying health and well-being that could make possible long-term survival and shared prosperity for all. Civilization is "bad medicine," and the longer it is practised the more it endangers everyone and brings the world ever closer to the brink of self-destruction.

Indigenous populations have remained very small and are marginalized in terms of wealth and power. It will be incumbent on settler populations who have lost connection with their Indigenous roots to make efforts to recover understanding and to take actions in support of re-Indigenization efforts. The help of allies will be critical.

NINE

NEEDING ALLIES

GRASPING THE FUTURE

For those concerned about the coming reckoning, it is imperative that major changes need to be made urgently. There is no time to lose. Some prognosticators say that we need more of the same to get us out of our mess—more science, greater technology, and increased artificial intelligence. But this book contends that the solution is there before our eyes—it is the Indigenous paradigm that has already successfully carried humanity for over 200,000 years, causing minimal damage to the environment or to one another. Radical changes are required to all facets of society, but a roadmap will become clearer once Indigenous philosophy and ways are fully understood and respected. But Indigenous Peoples, for all of the solutions they can provide, are far from having the political or economic clout to make much of an impact. This is where non-Indigenous peoples, who are willing to reclaim their lost Aboriginal wisdom, can become allies.

The future of humanity will hinge upon our ability to recover and restore Indigeneity. It was as recently as the 1820s, a mere two hundred years ago, that Indigenous people were still the majority of the world population. During that time, world population has more than quadrupled, increasing from 1.5 billion people to almost 8 billion in 2022. Along with this, banking, technology, industry, transport, nationalism, militarism, and environmental damage have expanded, exacerbated by the colonization of Indigenous Peoples and their lands. The victimized have every reason to feel bitter about what has happened to them: dispossession of their lands and undermining of their heritage—violence that continues to this day. It is only their conviction about their beliefs that impels them to continue to maintain positive relationships, promote healing, and maintain the strength to carry on.

At some point, the newcomers have to recognize the wrongness of their ways, and that the root of the problem has to do with a rejection of original spirituality. It was prophesized that Indigenous Peoples would show the way, but if the newcomers did not listen, the human world would end. If the worst excesses of civilization occurred within the last two hundred years, it will take at least as much energy and time to reverse course, unwinding damaging mentalities and technologies. It may take thousands of years to fully correct and turn things around, just as it took thousands of years to go off course with civilization.

ARRESTING GROWTH

In regions such as Europe and North America, constant economic growth is no longer advisable as social, ecological, and personal costs mount. Economic growth depends on social and geographic exploitation along with its unsustainable drain of materials and energy. At current rates of "ideal" 3 percent annual growth, the global economy will end up ten times larger by the end of this century.[142] The obvious axiom that nothing can grow indefinitely has been ignored as the desire for perpetual growth became an article of faith. This situation is exacerbated by the concealing of such costs, shielding investors from accountability, and passing damages onto future generations. Current accounting systems are shifting costs and damages to distant environments and people, delaying us from tackling challenges such as the climate crisis head-on.

Individualism is a deeply embedded societal characteristic. It leads to undermining the social fabric through competition and limiting access to common resources for shared well-being. The expression of individuality and its attendant preference for private homes is a boon for economic growth, fuelling the construction of more residences, each with its own furniture, refrigerator, heating system, etc. It's a gluttonously wasteful use of resources. And along with individualism could also come isolation, stress, overwork, illness, income insecurity, and substance abuse.

Socioeconomic systems established over the past few centuries encourage the continual reinvestment of money to beget ever more profit. Money provides the combustion for civilization's economic engine. "In the context of current institutions, what does appear capable of growing without limits is money....Without the constraint of gold or other material basis, the world's money supply is simply a set of numbers, spiralling out of control into a bad infinity that can only culminate in devaluation and destruction. For thousands of years, human societies have managed symbolic systems involving money. Although the abstract quality of money makes it susceptible to multiplication, money systems certainly do not require growth to function."[143]

The drive for endless growth coincides with the emergence of colonialism, beginning in the 1600s. Banks and government policies facilitated the rapid economic expansion that resulted from unfettered access to Indigenous lands and resources across the globe. Current economic models of capitalism, socialism, and communism all still embrace expansionism, upon which they depend for growth. For example, under growth targets in Russia, Khrushchev set an objective of 150 percent growth in a decade. But by the 1970s, economic growth in North America began to stagnate. This led to urgent strategies to restore growth:

> Ever since mid-century growth began to stagnate in the 1970s, governments have tried to minimize production costs by limiting wages, cutting benefits and public services, and weakening unions and labor standards. Meanwhile, they stimulated consumption with mechanisms like home mortgages and student loans that encourage workers to buy with credit. Starting in the 1980s, the UK, US and other economies were aggressively re-engineered via neoliberal reforms designed to rekindle growth for the wealthy, with the promise that prosperity would "trickle down" to the rest. Portrayed as liberating markets from burdensome restraints, neoliberal policies are anything but laissez-faire; they redirect regulations, taxes, and public spending on multiple scales.[144]

Yet purchasing power in the United States has not increased significantly over the same period, despite a three-fold growth in GDP; but personal debt has. In the United States during the 2008 financial crisis, ownership of fourteen million homes was lost. Political responses to shortages are now resorting to more resource extraction, national protectionism, cutting programs to serve the poor, and authoritarianism, such as increased policing.

It is a mystery to financiers how Indigenous Peoples of the Americas survived without currencies. Perhaps it was because they preferred to preserve the real value of goods, as opposed to economics that artificially inflated them. Indigenous Peoples viewed the natural world as an invaluable source of sustenance, rather than something to be exploited for the money and power. The environment sustained people—people did not have to sustain the environment. But what happens when the primary rationale for the system begins to change, and when there are no longer easy places to exploit new resources? Will this create new problems, including unfair distribution of wealth, disappearance of jobs, and devaluation of money? As it turns out, the artificial monetary economy will not be as reliable as the commons of ancient times. Being a useful instrument during times of rapid expansion, capitalism may well have now outlived its utility.

CHALLENGING CIVILIZATION

The biggest question of all is whether this monstrosity called civilization can be tamed. Writing this is not meant to imply that humanity needs to go back to living in huts and hunting with bows and arrows. The intellectual and technological advances made over past centuries cannot simply be forgotten or swept under the rug. They will need to be reviewed through the lens of wisdom and revised. A lot will need to be discarded: innumerable institutions and inventions that have been created by a materialistic society in its giddy quest for riches and power and built on the exploitation of nature and need to militarily defend what it has. The development of technologies that contribute to the ruination of nature, or are made for the killing of competitors or out of simple curiosity or for needless entertainment, all needs to be questioned.

The future goal for humanity needs to be to find the ways to return to balance with the environment and with each other. Solutions include recognition of the vital importance of spiritual values such as humility, honesty, respect, generosity, courage, love, and wisdom. These are matters of fundamental behaviour and morality. It will be incumbent upon religions to recognize the legitimacy of Indigenous ontology and that such spirituality is just as, if not more, foundational than scriptures or doctrines.

Attitudes about who we are, what our purpose for being is, and how we are to behave have to be re-examined by philosophers, intellectuals, and religious officials. Scholars need to assess how their interpretations have ignored Indigenous wisdom and practices. It needs to be admitted that civilization was a radical departure from Indigenous ways that existed for millennia. There needs to be an acknowledgement that secular approaches to learning are barren of spiritual content and that this contributes to our malaise today.

How can we return to a balance with nature? And how can the immense damages done to nature over centuries be restored? The very nature of contemporary lifestyles demands widespread exploitation of natural resources in order to support growth and the maintenance of populations and infrastructure. Is it possible to slow down and reverse this pattern? Is it possible to re-vision our way of life? Indigenous ways enhance rather than diminish the natural world. Can the mentality of settlers who recently came to the Americas shift to focus on the well-being of the environment instead of just constantly taking from it?

These are profound and monumental questions that cannot be tackled until there is a realization that taking the path of civilization has been to our great detriment. Politicians, rather than catering to the whims of the populace, need to show leadership by bringing in wise new policies. The general public needs to accept that great sacrifices will have to be made in order to heal the environment and relationships among ourselves. Resources and energies devoted to exploitation and military aggression or defence need to be rechannelled into social and cultural activities that promote cohesion and mental health. Then there is perhaps the greatest challenge of all: decreasing world human population.

Will it be possible to realize such changes? Looking to the past indicates that social change is laboriously difficult and frustratingly slow. People need to become aware of and support the changes. This can take generations, time that humanity, given the deteriorating conditions of the world, may simply not have. History seems to suggest that changes on such a scale are more than likely to occur only under duress—seismic activity, climatic changes, economic collapse, or worse, nuclear war. Indigenous Peoples have knowledge of the ways that people and the natural world can be systematically and steadily healed through spirituality.

CHANGING POLICIES

Civilization is still only recent in terms of the breadth of modern human history. Its longevity remains unproven. Some people become wealthier in the short run, but over time most are impoverished due to destruction of the natural world. Adhering to greed eventually brings struggle, suffering, and collapse. Building a human-centred society has been a monumental project, one that involved an immense amount of blood and tears to create our artificial environment. One of the solutions to escape the dynamic of civilization is to "de-grow."

Given that the species most similar to ourselves should be expected to survive for another 800,000 years, we need to think seriously about how we are going to go that distance. Indigenous people were in it for the long haul, having a strategy that would enable humanity to survive for hundreds of thousands of years. There was an emphasis on creating positive relations not only between humans socially but also with the environment and, most importantly, with the supernal. They understood that social and cultural assets are more valuable than economic capital.

The degrowth movement aims to purposefully slow down development in a planned way in order to minimize harm to the environment and people.[145] Is it possible to demobilize parts of the economy while securing the provisioning of basic goods and services, and to simultaneously find meaning in life? Degrowth guides people to re-establish societies based on mutual aid and care, reorienting pursuits away from individualism and profit and toward well-being and equity:[146]

> We seek to learn from common modes of production and consumption including communal food gardens, community supported agriculture, and agroecology networks; eco-communes, co-living and co-housing arrangements; peer to peer software, and digital commons; and co-parenting and childcare circles.[147]

> The concept of degrowth seeks to liberate peoples' time and energy to engage life journeys with patience, compassion, and care for self and others, rather than desperately working more and buying more to escape the pain, sadness, and frustration of finding meaning in the face of life's vulnerability.[148]

People collaboratively create, sustain, and enjoy shared resources via communication, regulation, mutual support, conflict negotiation, and experimentation. Meaning and pleasure can be obtained through activities such as song, dance, sport, prayer, sharing meals, conversation, and enjoying the natural environment. There are already individuals in the mainstream who are modest in their wants and find contentment mainly in family and friends. Many producers are conscious of and careful not to waste. Degrowth does not automatically replace capitalism, but rather coexists with it while long-term change occurs. Technology can continue to help manage and organize affairs. The economy will be more decentralized and small scale. Power dynamics related to race, gender, or class will be reduced and eventually eliminated.[149] Criticisms that people will not perfectly follow these principles should not discourage progress, as contradictions will be unavoidable.[150]

A green approach, including reaching net zero greenhouse gas emissions and clean air and water, combined with degrowth will address economic and environmental issues simultaneously,. This differs from the so-called "green economy" in that there is no further commercial expansion. There will be renewable energy, decarbonisation of transport, zero-carbon housing, and reforestation, and a fair distribution of costs and benefits. Sectors, such as energy, can be brought under public control and dividends will go towards mitigating climate deterioration. Sectors that overuse and destroy the natural environment would be heavily taxed. Banks would invest in the new economy to help bring about universal incomes, restoring the commons, reducing working hours, and stabilizing the environment. In other words, it is a slow and gradual process that will require a high degree of public cooperation.

There will inevitably be anti-degrowth forces fuelled by a public afraid of disruptive change. Unrest due to rapid change can be avoided by building alliances, creating alternatives to market economies, and deconstructing dominant systems.[151] International organizations such as the United Nations will be indispensable to facilitate and coordinate such an initiative. Allies can be found in sectors including education, media, social activists, hospitals, science, and medicine, as well as business. Indeed, 70 percent of people surveyed in twenty-nine countries agree overconsumption is putting the planet at risk and that they could do with less. Promoting well-being needs to be emphasized, and radicalism is to be avoided as it will only produce backlash.

Done carefully and systematically, factors can work synergistically to avoid disruption by controlling the flow of money, supporting community currencies, and issuing public funding for desired goals. There is potential to work with Indigenous communities that are naturally more ideologically aligned. There can also be dialogue with poorer countries whose resources currently tend to benefit wealthy nations. Ironically, the authors of the degrowth movement note that it is probably easier to imagine the end of the world than the end of growth.[152]

However, a fatal shortcoming of the degrowth movement is that it is based upon a rationalist approach, one that does not incorporate spirituality in any meaningful way. It is one thing to argue and convince people that something needs to be done, but it is another to get them to do it. Inevitably, some groups will game the system, utilizing the degrowth movement in ways that will increase their own advantage. In other words, if basic virtues such as humility, honesty, respect, and generosity have not been effectively ingrained in the population, the degrowth movement is inevitably destined to fail. Bringing about such a wholesale change in hearts and attitudes does not occur overnight. Civilization will need to abandon the human-centric attitudes that got it in this dilemma to begin with.

Virtually all nations have adopted wetiko behaviours of resource exploitation and environmental destruction for economic gain. At the same time, it is necessary to recognize that the vast majority of individual citizens do not necessarily subscribe to the scourge of greed. Many individuals value healthy relationships, appreciate the existence of plants and animals, and are sensitive to the needs of the environment. They still carry their ancient heritage in their genes. But they are hopelessly stuck in the system. Elders at the First Nations University of Canada counsel students to "take the best of both worlds" while retaining a personal foundation of Indigenous values. In other words, an Indigenous person can live in wetiko society, but one must preserve one's identity and values by remaining mindful of one's spiritual responsibilities.

SPIRITUALIZING KNOWLEDGE SYSTEMS

Mainstream science, as we accept it now, is extremely recent in terms of a modern human presence that dates back 200,000 years. It is charitably said that science facilitates the process of learning, understanding, synthesizing, revising, and repeating the process for a better knowledge of the world. For the Greeks, it reflected a preoccupation with understanding what they perceived as a chaotic physical world. Apart from such generic and generous explanations, it must also be admitted that some of the primary drivers for modern scientific research include curiosity and ego, the quest for profit and wealth, and the exigencies of war.

As an Indigenous intellectual, there is an obligation to ask further questions. What was the notion of Indigenous knowledge that existed previously? Surely there must have been a concerted effort to relate to the natural environment. What form might this have taken? The obvious problem that emerges from modern science, which is based upon rationalism, secularism, and materialism, is the absence of recognition of spirit and of our sacred responsibility of stewardship. As a result, mainstream science misses an important component that could greatly influence both its approaches and outcomes.

Looking at Indigenous epistemology, the following would apply in terms of an approach to "science": Indigenous Peoples recognized the spirit in and integrity of all created things; they did not believe that they were entitled to dominate or abuse other parts of creation; there is a belief that humans should not interfere with or exploit other creatures; and finally, any relationship with the natural world should be pursued at a spiritual level. We know that Indigenous Peoples were perfectly capable of observing and manipulating their environment. Apart from discoveries in mathematics, astronomy and architecture, Indigenous Peoples of the Americas are noted as having produced what is probably the greatest inventory of edible plants and usable medicines ever known. A partial list includes beans, corn, chocolate, maple syrup, peanuts, peppers, pineapple, potatoes, pumpkins, quinoa, squash, sunflowers, vanilla, and wild rice. There were various herbal medicines and anaesthetics, including aspirin and quinine. Other inventions and technologies include astronomy, calendars, canoes, mathematics, pyramids, rubber, and writing systems. Mainstream scholars cite such developments as proof that the Indigenous Peoples of the Americas were on the same path that would have inevitably have led to the Euro-American model that is now the world standard. However, these developments were all made from a perspective of spirituality that did not condone unwise exploitation of the environment.

Is it possible that Indigenous Peoples took another approach to science, basing it upon connecting to spirit consciousness through ceremonies and protocols? African intellectual and Indigenous healer Malidoma Some would say yes:

> Science is the investigation of the spirit world more than the world of the physical....What in the West might be regarded as fiction, among the Dagara is believed as fact, for we have seen it with our eyes, heard it with our ears, or felt it with our own hands....My civilized mind was in fact a rather narrow mind....Westerners tried to control magic by insisting on knowing a visible cause for anything...Different laws operate in the different dimensions of reality. Ritual is the technology that allows the manipulation of these subtle energies.[153]

The primary instrument of exploration was consciousness itself, and the observable and verifiable results were corroborated through individual experience. As noted before, distinguished scholar Vine Deloria recounted reports made by reputable sources of unusual occurrences such as the ability to locate lost people or objects at a long distance, the ability to communicate with plants, the ability to communicate with animals, the ability to enable plants to fully grow within hours, and the ability to quickly heal severe wounds. Art Napoleon confirmed that someone who is "gifted" is generally recognized as having spirit guides that can be called upon for a variety of reasons, and can sometimes alter the natural order.[154]

Entrepreneurs, such as Elon Musk, face impossible odds in figuring out how to live on Mars or even to travel to planets that may be light years away. At the same time, there is a great deal of conversation today about UFOs (or Unidentified Aerial Phenomena) and speculation about aliens. Elders tell me that they believe there are beings on other planets. Even the Pope says he would welcome aliens. My mentor Danny Musqua noted our fascination about travelling into space and how we are able to conceptualize space travel. But, he told me, people will travel not in physical spaceships but rather in psychic ones created by our minds. Is that perhaps the real technology to travel the universe? Perhaps there are places in the cosmos where beings with consciousness similar to ours chose to continue following the Creator's instructions and, in doing so, did not pursue self-destructive ways. Perhaps, after many thousands of years focused on spiritual development, humankind could have mastered travelling by using the tools of the 95 percent of what exists (dark matter and dark energy). This would give us a real connection to the rest of the universe, and offer clues on an even better way science could be approached.

PROPHECY

The Seven Fires prophecy of the Anishinaabe (or Ojibway) (see Appendix), sometimes called the Seven Generations prophecy, foresaw the arrival of newcomers who would damage the Indigenous world. It also prophesized the need to return to Indigenous ways. Crises such as climate change will hopefully soon bring humanity to accept that the current system has reached its limit. Civilization has been a monumental human project, but it is ultimately doomed to failure. In the post-civilization stage, what will take its place?

The Seven Fires prophecy has been passed down by a succession of Knowledge Keepers. The early parts (fires) of the prophecy deal with the movement of their people as they moved west following visions and dreams about where they could live. Each of these fires was an epoch in the evolution of their society. The latter part of the prophecy recounts the arrival of fair-skinned people who do not share Indigenous ways. The prophecy recounts the devastation brought by the newcomers, and of their need to heal by reconciling their ways. Returning to Indigenous philosophy and ways will lead to a return of healthy and happy times. Pursuing their current course of materialism will lead to the destruction of all. This prophecy contains wisdom that all need to take seriously.

The United Nations Declaration on the Rights of Indigenous Peoples (UNDRIP), hard-won over decades of lobbying, recognizes that wrongs have been committed against Original Peoples. The declaration was approved on September 13, 2007, with the support of 144 countries of the United Nations General Assembly. Australia, Canada, New Zealand, and the United States initially voted against the resolution over uncertainty as to how it would impact existing laws and control of resources, but all four have since conditionally dropped their opposition.

Article 12.1 of UNDRIP states: "Indigenous peoples have the right to manifest, practice, develop, and teach their spiritual and religious traditions, customs and ceremonies." Unfortunately, the declaration remains largely a hollow gesture. It is lofty in its goals, but it has no force in law and no ability for recourse to international courts, as tribal peoples are not recognized as nations. It serves as guidance only and, even if implemented, will never go far enough to repair all the damage. How each nation deals with Indigenous issues is left up to that jurisdiction. The vast majority are simply not motivated to make changes they perceive as diminishing their national sovereignty or economy.[155]

President Evo Morales of Bolivia, a Quechua, was the first leader to fully embrace UNDRIP. His government has sought to respect nature by granting rivers similar rights to humans. The move is driven by Indigenous Peoples who contend that "we belong to a big family of plants and animals" and that Mother Earth is "sacred, fertile and the source of life that feeds and cares for all human beings."[156]

NEEDING ALLIES

Those wishing to restore the world to healthy balance need to support existing Indigenous societies and assist them through any means, whether that be moral, educational, political, or financial. Allies are those who have come to appreciate Indigenous spirituality and thinking, and who understand the importance of these ways. They recognize that all of our ancestors were once Indigenous. Many peoples have adopted modern life with varying degrees of reticence, or as a result of being forced to over the past few centuries. They may even retain cultural elements of their Indigenous past. Allies can lend their moral, political, economic, and social influence to help mainstream society make the difficult, complicated and arduous changes in their thinking, public institutions, and economic systems. They will respect that Indigenous Peoples will play the leading role.

World re-Indigenization will have fertile ground where there are still remaining pockets of Indigenous culture. However, there needs to be receptivity on the part of mainstream authorities to pursue such policies. It will be important to recognize the relentless efforts of civilization's proponents to discredit Indigenous ways. One must respect the notion that humans are capable of overcoming pride, hatred, lying, greediness, cowardice, hatred, and stupidity. If not, then the human race is definitely doomed. Is it possible that educational institutions can teach such values as effectively as they are capable of teaching reading, writing, and arithmetic? There needs to be a genuine global effort to recognize that in every corner of the world there have been Indigenous cultures, many of which still thrived up until mere centuries ago. Why would it not be possible to rediscover and revive those traditions? It may begin in ways as simple as art, craft, music, and dance. There also has to be recognition of the positive value to humanity of such cultural activity. It may not lead to a wealthy or powerful lifestyle, but it can result in healthiness, happiness, and security for the future.

CULTIVATING ALLIANCES

The public needs knowledge and education about Indigenous Peoples in order to gain empathy towards their brethren. As knowledge and awareness and reconciliation grow, it is paramount that the youth be exposed to the story of Indigenous *ecolizations*, their ways of thought, and their practices. Young people are more open-minded and capable of recognizing the intrinsic value of these ideas and their importance for the survival of humanity over the long term.

In terms of trust, there have always been dangers of appropriation and the co-opting of Indigenous culture and knowledge for profit or influence. Only through the rigorous following of spiritual protocols can allies earn a position of trust. One example of a country trying to break that mold is Bhutan, which uses gross national happiness instead of gross domestic product as a measure of national performance—a way of attaining meaning and fulfillment in harmony with Buddhist spiritual values.

There is no crystal ball for the future, other than realizing that, as human beings, we are charting our course and are fully accountable for what happens down the road. Indigenous Peoples always placed a priority on leaving a better environment for future generations. How long humanity survives will depend on whether we can truly embrace that ethos again.

TEN

THE ONLY VIABLE PATH

SEEING CLEARLY

The evidence covered in my series of three books on Indigenous spirituality, including this one, should deliver a clear message: there was nothing wrong with Indigenous belief in the first place. The reason for its decline was hostility from others who thought that humans should occupy a more central role in the created world. This was an abandonment of Indigenous wisdom and ideology, and it permitted humankind to unwisely pursue numerous avenues of self-interest.

It should be obvious by now that it was an enormous blunder to discredit Indigenous knowledge and ways. The root source of today's malaise is not so much colonialism, or racism, but rather the adoption of hostile ideologies. In a world where respect and generosity have been lost, it is not a surprise that the "civilized" refuse to accept that the "uncivilized" ever had anything worthwhile to contribute. Or perhaps they simply think that Indigenous Peoples are free to follow their ways, but that theirs is not a progressive choice. Worse, some will be jaded, believing that even if Aboriginal Peoples are right, it is too late and too onerous to change things.

It is certainly true that civilization's momentum has handily overthrown the Indigenous world, and that one of the most difficult things of all is to persuade people that this has all been wrong. This is particularly true of religion. However, everyone needs to recognize their moral responsibility to correct past wrongs and rectify matters for future generations. Considering the alternatives, it should be abundantly clear that a return to original wisdom is the only viable path to recover a healthy future. This will only be possible with the support of allies and their ability to bring about change from within the mainstream.

Given humanity's current dangerous trajectory, things are not going well. It would be wonderful to have a crystal ball that could foretell the future, but it is clear that our human footprint is suffocating and destroying the life systems that support us. It is likely that our actions will cause irreversible global heating that will result in the mass extinction of species, including our own. In the face of this looming challenge, we need to realize that, while our actions may have initially appeared to be clever and beneficial for humankind, they were in fact an aberration and a danger. Ancestors have been dismissed as being misguided and under the thrall and control of nature. It needs to be recognized that Indigenous Peoples, berated as ignorant, backward, and unprogressive, did indeed have the philosophies that would enable humanity to thrive for another 800,000 years.[157] Were their simple approaches of nurturing nature, promoting healthy relationships, and deepening understanding of the supernatural not the formula that could carry us that far?

DISMAL FUTURE

Futurists are raising the alarm. Theodore Gordon observes, "We are shocked by surprises, unwanted consequences of our behavior, unanticipated results, formerly the unrecognized effects. We are victims of an untamed future that forces us to run harder and faster as we sense we are getting further and further behind, battered by crisis after crisis."[158] Ross Dawson worries, "The most important question facing humanity is whether we have the collective ability to respond to accelerating change in a world in which short-sighted actions over many decades have created extraordinary challenges for us."[159] Rodrigo Nieto-Gomez observes, "Even though this is a time of technological abundance and living conditions are better than they have ever been in the history of humankind, you would not know this by listening to the news or talking with the fearful ethnic majorities that are driving the political conversations of the global north."[160]

Has the technology we have produced really led to what our children truly need? Rick Sax notes, "The irony is that our scientific triumphs over the 50 years since the publication of *Future Shock* continue to be subverted by our own cravings, folly, hubris, and evolutionary hardwiring. We are still a long way from achieving Toffler's grandest rose-coloured aspiration, that the 'super-industrial revolution' could erase hunger, homelessness, disease, ignorance and brutality."[161] David Weinberger wonders, "If the internet's information overload left us on the verge of psychosis, why did we flock to it, and tout it as a positive transformative abundance?"[162]

Futurists note that "progress" has allowed us to do more—but they also question whether we have focussed on the things that really matter. This is particularly true about our faith in computers and artificial intelligence (AI). Techno-optimist John Smart represents a lot of experts who believe AI is the answer for humanity. But their view is exactly that—one of experts whose knowledge will rarely filter down to common consciousness:

> Many of us look to the future, congratulating ourselves on seeing that modern progress is no longer linear, but exponential, and then make the mistake of expecting the world will continue its current gentle exponential rates of change. But it won't…Scientific, technical, and economic change are actually superexponential at the leading edge of complexity. Certain changes compound and converge on each other.…A wall of change is coming towards us at present. So, we must learn to think both superexponentially and developmentally.…When we recognize that the heart of adaptation is understanding and advancing interdependence, via better ethics and empathy, we can keep human needs and problems at the centre of our foresight. If this view of the world is applied well, it should cause us to be less selfish and aggressive in pursuing our own desires, and more concerned with the needs of the group.[163]

The flaw, as usual, in Smart's approach is that it is purely rationalistic and lacks the essence of spirituality. It is now more important than ever to reconsider our purpose by revisiting ancient understanding and wisdom. To say that there is an urgency to "turn the ship around" is an understatement indeed!

PROUD TO BE UNCIVILIZED

Ecolizations were unprepared to counteract non-Indigenous ideology and its agenda of conquest and colonization. Diseases that spread from Europe decimated original populations. Finally, Indigenous Peoples would not resist by matching the deceit, cruelty, and barbarity of the invaders, as that would require abandonment of their own cherished values.

Change has dramatically accelerated since the Industrial Revolution of the early 1800s. Overpopulation of the earth, stress on the natural environment, and catastrophic effects of climate change are bringing things to a head. Yet humanity continues to live in a bubble perpetuated by the illusion of material prosperity and technological comfort. Efforts by world governments to solve problems are so impotent that they verge on the farcical. Only higher spiritual authority can bring universal order. In order to recognize what is occurring, one needs to look not just at yearly or even decade-long results but rather at the long spans of centuries and millennia. The results, for those who are paying attention, should be alarming.

Remember, Indigenous Peoples regard their sacred duty as one of respect for creation and living in harmony. The action of placing humanity and its selfish interests above all else was a critical mistake. It resulted in a misleading ideology that has critical implications for the destiny of humankind. Elder Oren Lyons observed,

> The spiritual side of the natural world is absolute. The laws are absolute. Our instructions, and I'm talking about for all human beings, our instructions are to get along. Understand what these laws are. Get along with the laws and help them and work with them. We are

told a long time ago that if you do that, life is endless. It just continues on in great cycles of regeneration, great powerful cycles of life regenerating and regenerating and regenerating.[164]

The success, power, and health of each cycle builds upon previous cycles, increasingly strengthening the vitality of the life. Mainstream academics rarely appreciate the simple potency of Indigenous philosophy. The cyclical view of history is not "anti-evolutionary." If one looks carefully, one will realize that events in nature are cyclical rather than linear. It applies to individuals and to collective societies as they revisit events of the previous day, season, or year. Even species and planets have their cycles.

The "uncivilized" are sensitive to the spirit world and respectful of ancestors. They acknowledge and respect the rights of plants and animals and other created beings to exist without interference. In this way, they avoid the worst excesses of the civilized, including inequality and environmental destruction. Are they improperly labelled "primitive"?

In Indigenous Eden, ceremonies, prayer, and healing produced healthy and happy societies. Fearing the unknown was the first failing of civilization, which no longer trusted the benevolence of the Creator. In abandoning Indigenous knowledge, humanity has forgotten its original purpose on Earth—to learn to live in harmonious relationships. Instead, people have become increasingly hostile towards one another, crime becomes rampant, and there appears to be no bottom to the depth of depravity that can occur.

REMEDYING PAST INJUSTICES

The Vatican bears a lot of responsibility for what happened to Indigenous Peoples across the globe. As King of Kings, only the Pope had the authority to give European monarchs permission to encroach on the lands of nonbelievers. The Vatican decided that it was legally justifiable to go forth and to not only save the souls but also claim their lands. The end result was wholesale slaughter of Aboriginal Peoples and dispossession of their sacred birthright.

Did things have to happen this way? Had the Vatican not intervened, explorers and traders would have lacked the authorization to overthrow Indigenous societies. The newcomers would have had to develop a relationship and gain greater understanding of the native inhabitants. Original Peoples were welcoming and hospitable, as this was their cultural practice. Europeans generally perceived their own ways as superior, something that had been deeply ingrained in them. But some would have been motivated to understand Indigenous ways and to embrace their culture. Granted, the epidemics would have invariably devastated Indigenous populations. And, even had many Europeans embraced Aboriginal ways, they would have eventually become vulnerable to attack by pirates and invaders from overseas.

Through its declaration of laws that legitimized the rampant invasion of Indigenous lands, the Vatican created a legal fiction for claiming sovereignty over those lands and original inhabitants. Had this structure not been created, Indigenous governments would have had to have been respected, leaving greater opportunity for Indigenous *ecolizations* to survive. The wholesale destruction of Indigenous societies and the confiscation of their possessions by Europeans gave an immense boost to the latter's ambitious quests for wealth and power. Colonization led to rampant conflict over control of Indigenous lands around the world. Indigenous wisdom would have called for respect between peoples and for welcoming visitors based upon positive relationships and healing, rather than conflict and subjugation.

The Pope appears to have renounced *terra nullius* as the basis for the continuing domination of Indigenous Peoples; however, he has also washed his hands of history, blaming governments for abusing that law. During Pope Francis's penitential journey to Canada in 2022, he promised to walk a new path with the Aboriginal population. It remains to be seen if he truly meant it. There is potential for reform in the Americas, as displacement of Indigenous Peoples and their ways is still relatively recent in world history.[165] The ability of newcomers to show that they appreciate and can learn from recent history will be key to future reforms.

RIGHT TO SURVIVE

Critics of Indigenous Peoples often say, "If you don't like civilization that much, why do you live in cities and enjoy modern technologies?" This is hypocrisy, they claim. However, from an Indigenous point of view, it is a matter of survival. We have the same right as anyone else to live by whichever means are necessary. If we are no longer able to live by the hunt and instead have to get an education and a job to make money, so be it. This does not have to mean giving up our basic beliefs and values. While we live in civilization, we can see through its weaknesses and avoid its worst pitfalls. If things were ever to reform to be more like the original ways, we would be the first to embrace it. Expecting Indigenous Peoples to return to the bush and live as they did five hundred years ago is simply another form of exclusion.

Indigenous Peoples would have eventually discovered all the current technological marvels, and even more, had they been given the time. But they would have done so with spiritual maturity and in a manner that would not harm or endanger ourselves and our other created relatives. If humanity is to survive for 1,000,000 years, as do our closest mammalian species, then the height of our accomplishment should occur around 500,000 years—our "middle age"—not at 200,000 years. At this point we are akin to an immature twenty-year-old. In other words, Indigenous Peoples were right to be "unproductive" as we worked on inner maturity rather than grasping wealth and power at the earliest opportunity.

Hope was not an Indigenous virtue because it was not necessary. Instead there was trust in the Creator and Its bountiful gifts to provide for a secure future. The human-made world pales in comparison to the overall miracle of creation and the time spans over which creatures have come and gone. It may take centuries and millennia to redo and reshape our current misguided systems, but this must be started quickly. Education can be a powerful tool in de-civilizing and re-Indigenizing. In education, the emphasis needs to be on teaching spiritual wisdom, more so than on rational thinking and facts. What good is it to produce scientists, physicians, economists, and artists if they do not have a sound moral foundation? The only ultimate source and authority for proper behaviour that all of humanity can respect can come only from one source: Kise-Manitow and the original instructions.

RESPECTING NATURAL LAW

Viewing civilizations as linear progressions leads one to false assumptions that there are never-ending resources, that military power needs to be constantly increased, and that human longevity can be extended indefinitely. Some scholars suggest that the march from hunter-gatherer societies to contemporary "advanced" globalized economies is an immutable law of progress. In reality, it is a poor choice. Indigenous

Peoples suffer, and continue to sacrifice, in order to remind humanity of its original spiritual mandate.

The reality is that death ultimately overtakes every living thing. New life miraculously and mysteriously reappears. The cycle of human life on Earth will not last forever, and even the planet itself has a fixed time span. It may well be the case that humanity, unable to learn the basic lessons, will end its cycle ignominiously. Because humanity has chosen exploitation, with its downward spirals of unhealed relationships and increasingly toxic environment, human life may be short—a mere blink of the eye in earthly time.

I used to debate with fellow academics whether or not Indigenous cultures would inevitably all go along the path of modern civilizations. Many of them are adamant that this is the natural course of events. Precivilized societies are simply assumed to be civilizations-in-the-making. Of course, they took this position because of the way in which they interpret the entirety of human experience through the lens of rationalism and science. Fundamental to this argument is an assumption that humans are born inherently and hopelessly self-centred, greedy, and violent. This was certainly true of the purportedly great civilizations of the Greeks and Romans. Revealing the truth are Indigenous *ecolizations* that still carry on today, living in a humble manner and avoiding self-destructive behaviour.

GUIDANCE FOR THE FUTURE

What, then, are the lessons that Indigenous wisdom can provide for our future? We need to recognize ancient Indigenous heritage and that it provided a solid foundation for the 99 percent of human existence prior to the turning point of the 1820s. The humility, patience, selflessness, and courage with which humans survived for tens of thousands of years has been totally devalued because it was not perceived as contributing anything to human growth. However, what these ancient peoples, and those Indigenous Peoples who today continue to honour original ways, provided was an attitude of respect and reverence for the Earth, which was seen as a vessel that had the potential to thrive indefinitely if properly tended. This meant not allowing human self-interest and greed to come to the fore—something that our peoples dreaded in the form of wetiko. We knew that spirit of greed, once out of control, would totally and fatally consume its victim.

In this book, civilization is described as the rejection and abandonment an Age of Indigenous Wisdom that had flourished for over 190,000 years. The delicate balance between Manitow and humans, and amongst humans and all other beings, could only be held so long as humans agreed to abide by their responsibilities. These included recognizing that we are allowed on the planet in order to learn, and to not start seeing the Earth's abundance as a cookie jar from which to take as much as we want.

The embrace of civilization was not such a popular option, as it was not until the 1820s that its adherents outnumbered Indigenous Peoples. In retrospect, many in today's mainstream are there because they were subjugated, enslaved, converted, or dispossessed—they had no other choice. Over the years, triumph over triumph—amassing of untold wealth, creation of vast armies, dominion over global empires, invention of life-altering technologies, and thinking we understand the universe through astronomy—have led humanity to believe that we are truly something special. In our hubris, we proclaim ourselves to be all-powerful—even capable of populating the universe. In this mindset, humanity does not see the need to believe in a Creator. But despite all of this bluster, are we just actually a group of beings who don't really understand why we are living? We think we are doing well because we have feathered our nest with so many conveniences, but in reality are we simply oblivious to the damage being inflicted upon our life support systems? Will catastrophic climate change, among the many other insults to the natural world, ending up driving humanity off of the planet?

How would the world have been different had Indigenous ways not been destroyed? In the Indigenous practice of stewardship, wildlife and plant resources could have continued to thrive and provide ample resources for the common benefit of a population that remained in respectful balance with nature. Indigenous Peoples proved that access to common resources is possible without the need for boundaries, individual property, money, or police forces. Values of humility, honesty, generosity, courage, love, and wisdom were all that were required. Some may think that this analysis is simplistic. However, the fact is that the conditions that have led to our present world have been the result of choices, not the least of which has been the dismissing of Indigenous knowledge. The stakes involved are very real, critical, and have imminent consequences.

IS GLOBAL REFORM POSSIBLE?

A growing community of scientists, environmentalists, and philosophers argue that we are already well into the terminal phase of civilization. Elon Musk, Stephen Hawking, and others have expressed their concern that there is a self-destruct button inherent in technological culture that can annihilate every advanced life form. Is this why civilizations could not signal their presence to the rest of the universe? They either blew themselves up, poisoned their environment, or were over-taken by soulless artificial intelligence? Looking around at our current mess, this possibility does not seem particularly far-fetched.

The wetiko cultures that are now in control of world affairs pre-tend to solve these problems through a combination of rationalism, economic development, and military threat. Unfortunately, they lack spiritual authority and will never possess it until they reconcile with Indigenous Peoples and their ancient wisdom. Only a moral revolu-tion can bring humanity back to its original path. What if we could redirect our intellectual, economic, and technological energies into healing Earth? This would lead us closer to a future that recognizes, celebrates, and honours the higher nature of our species.

Reconciliation with Indigenous Peoples will need to begin with an admission that Indigenous beliefs are more holistic and provide wise guidance. Spiritual leaders are guides, not infallible authorities. In traditional communities, whenever differences in beliefs arose, the first recourse was to join together in prayer and ceremony. That way, individual egos and pride were left at the door, and respectful dia-logue under authority of the supernal could occur. Those involved in the debate would discuss the meanings of their dreams, visions, and meditations until consensus was reached. The genius of spirituality as a higher form of intelligence was able to assert itself, as the answers often came from a source that was over and above the machinations of the rational mind alone.

Indigenous philosophy and worldview challenge the heart and soul of civilization. Not until people recognize that every insect and blade of grass has equal value will we be capable of living in harmony with nature. Humanity needs to confront one of its most intractable issues—admitting that our numbers have become too great, now at least five times greater than they should be in order to sustain balance with nature. Unfortunately, such change goes against every political and economic instinct of governments, which thrive on meeting the whims of their populations. Can the world's nations devise a sophisticated and effective strategy that does not harm the planet? Greater advances can be made through intimate interaction, understanding, and cooperation with nature, rather than the heavy-handed and arbitrary forcing of nature to bend to human will. People's inability to deal meaningfully with critical issues lays bare the immaturity of humanity in its current phase of evolution.

At this stage, governments need to contemplate how they can move into a post-civilization mode. It will be a tall order. This will be far more difficult than the pursuit of civilization that has been occurring over the past several centuries. The great motivators of acquiring wealth and power and the egotistic rewards of individual achievement and greater comfort have predominated. Undoing all of the accumulated damages will entail great sacrifices and suffering as mainstream society rediscovers the values of humility, honesty, and wisdom. It will take double the effort, probably over thousands of years, to put the genie of civilization back in the bottle and to keep it there.

OUR ULTIMATE DESTINY

When mosôm Danny first told me that our people came from the stars, I thought this must just be a figure of speech. How could we have come from the stars? Mosôm was very matter-of-fact about this statement. Moreover, these are sacred accounts, not fairy tales. In retrospect, I realized that mosôm had prepared me for such ideas during our discussions about the reality and nature of spirit. Leaning towards me, he said:

I have to be careful to whom and where I give this information. That is what the old people tell us, so that is what I am doing. Because of that, I am not afraid to tell you…You will find a set of values and teachings that you have been looking for, and find answers for, because it is meant for you to find these answers. It is meant for you to share these answers.[166]

I replied that I was very honoured that he placed such confidence in me. Mosôm explained that we are originally spirit beings who wanted to experience physical life. So we asked Kise-Manitow for permission and were granted it, albeit with strict admonitions. The plants and other already-existing inhabitants of Earth would accept, welcome, and help support us, but we had to respect them and behave as stewards.

But there was still something missing from the picture. How could we as humans have arrived here? Travel by physical spacecraft, by all accounts, is an impossibility given the incomprehensible distances and dangers involved. It was not on spaceships, mosôm reassured me, becoming very serious. He recounted the interest with which our ancestors greeted white peoples' inventions such as the car and the airplane. These were very strange things, they agreed, but wondered why these things were even necessary. Had not Manitow given people all the things they already needed to get around and to survive? But mosôm acknowledged one thing—that humans have great capacity for imagination and inventiveness.

Then he got to the real point: we did not come here on physical spaceships. This brought me back to elder teachings and old stories about how people were once able to travel in spirit form. They knew how to communicate with people at great distances without use of technology and how to find lost objects. They also communicated with ancestors and spirit helpers through ceremonies. We were capable of utilizing our transcendent consciousness. How we travelled to Earth, mosôm concluded, was by what is best described as psychic spaceships that we were able to create. Is this perhaps why, although our bodies are eminently suited for earthly survival, our consciousnesses are so out of synchronicity with the rest of the environment?

This got me wondering about aliens. Hollywood portrays aliens as dangerous and wanting to come to Earth to exploit humans. In our science fiction, we are anxious that hostile aliens with superior technology will invade our planet, enslave us, and seize all of our resources. In doing this are we in reality projecting ourselves, who are already the invaders and exploiters of the Earth and its plants and animals? If so, we don't have to fear aliens coming and exploiting us. We have already fulfilled that role. As for the UFOs that supposedly occasionally visit us—why don't they stop and visit if they are so concerned about our welfare? Is it perhaps that they already know who we are, how we behave, and what we have become?

It also makes sense that any extraterrestrial being that managed to find its way to Earth, covering light years of distance, would not be from a civilization. This is because civilization, being self-centred, antagonistic towards its surroundings, and bent on imposing its will on creation rather than living in harmony, will end up destroying itself. Aliens who can manage to come this far have been able to find their rightful place as denizens of the universe because they cooperated with the Creator's will and learned to harness its subtle powers. Aliens would not be greedy, hostile, or violent—instead, they would be highly morally evolved in their behaviour.

After a conversation regarding the destiny of humanity in this world, mosôm Danny confided that he felt humans are preparing to travel again:

If we destroy this earth, there will come a time when we will be able to fly up to those other worlds. We are at the edge of that time when the Creator and the grandfathers are preparing us to leave this world. ... It comes from the knowledge systems that the Creator has revealed to us, through our sciences he was preparing us to save ourselves from the destruction of this planet.[167]

Did he mean that our consciousness will transmigrate to another planet on psychic spacecraft, just as they came to Earth? I was reminded that there could potentially be eight billion Earth-like planets in the Milky Way galaxy alone, enough for one planet per every human on Earth.[168]

One hopes that humanity's sojourn on Earth will end up being dignified and meaningful. But then, if our consciousnesses are forced to move to another planet, will it be as lush and welcoming as Earth? It appears that we are writing our own story and creating our own destiny. Either we will be intelligent apes doomed to oblivion because of the Anthropocene, or we are spirit beings who are capable of travelling again to another physical realm in order to continue our learning journey. The bottom line is that the universe was not created just for humans. We are part of a much larger and mysterious creation. It is time to move into the post-civilization era and return to our Indigenous wisdom and ways. The choice of path is ours.

SEVEN FIRES PROPHECY

Excerpts taken from Sacred Instructions *by Sherri Mitchell*

The prophet of the First Fire told them that they would leave their homeland and travel west by sea to an island that was shaped like a turtle.[169] This island was a symbol for purification of the Earth, and it would be found at both the beginning and end of their journey. Along the way, they would stop seven times and establish villages, but their journey would only be complete when they reached a place where the food grew on the water (wild rice).

The prophet of the Second Fire told them that they would camp along the sweet water, and there they would lose their way, but they would receive dreams of a little boy that would set them back on the right or true path.

The prophet of the Third Fire told them that they would find the path to the lands that had been prepared for them, and they would indeed come to the place where the food grew on the water.

The prophet of the Fourth Fire came to them as two in the form of one. This symbolized the two faces of the light-skinned man that would come. The Anishinaabe would know their future based on the face that the light-skinned man showed to them. The first of the two prophets told them that if the light-skinned people came with a face of true brotherhood, it would be a beautiful time of wonder and shared knowledge, and their nations would join with others and become great, and all would benefit from this coming-together. The second of the two prophets told them that the light-skinned people had another face. At first this face may look like the face of brotherhood, but underneath it there was greed and deception. He told the Anishinaabe people that if they came bearing weapons and appeared to be suffering, then the face they showed would be the face of death, and it would lead to the poisoning of the waters and death of the animals.

The prophet of the Fifth Fire told them that the light-skinned people would be conflicted in their own minds and that they would be enmeshed in an ongoing struggle with the natural ways of the spirit and the nations of natural peoples on the Earth. This prophet also warned them that there would be those among the light-skinned people who would bring them a promise, wreathed in smiles and joy. This was a promise of salvation. If they took this promise, the people would be lost for generations to come, and those who accepted it would be nearly destroyed.

The prophet of the Sixth Fire told them that it would be during the time of the Sixth Fire that the promise of salvation would be proved to be false, and the people would see the destruction that it had brought to the people of the Earth. Those who had taken this promise and walked away from their traditional teachings and the ways of the Earth would be lost, and their children would be sick and dying.

The prophet of the Seventh Fire was young, and his eyes glowed from within. This prophet told them that there would come a time when the waters would be contaminated and all of the plants and animals that relied on those waters would become sick and begin to die. The forests and prairies would disappear and the air would become so clogged that it would lose the power of life. The way of thinking that was brought to the red, black, and yellow nations by the white nation would bring great danger to the entire Earth and threaten the continuation of all life. But during this time there would be a new people that would awaken from the clouds of illusion and come forward. Those people would retrace their steps and find the gifts that had been left for them on the path. Then the old teachings and old stories would come back to them, and they would remember their original instructions and become strong again in the ways of the circle.

These new people would seek out the Elders and they would ask for their guidance. Good elders would prove hard to find, many will have forgotten their own teachings and be unable to stop to help. Some elders would point them in the wrong direction, and others would be silent because there had been no one to hear their teachings for too long. Others would remain silent out of fear. If the new people learned to trust the ways of the circle and trained themselves to hear the inner voice, wisdom could return to them in waking and sleeping dreams, and the sacred fire would be lit once again. The light-skinned people would be given a choice of two paths. If they chose the correct path, then the Seventh Fire would be used to light the Eighth Fire, which would be a lasting fire of unity and peace. If they chose the wrong path, and stayed locked into their old mindset, the destruction they wrought would come back and destroy them, and all the people of the Earth would experience great suffering and death.

GLOSSARY

Anishinaabe (Saulteaux): First Nation prevalent around the Great Lakes, also called the Ojibway. Those who migrated onto the prairies during the fur trade and adopted plains culture are termed Saulteaux.

ceremonies: Spiritual practices intended to strengthen connection with the numinous and to promote healing.

commons: The concept that all resources such as wild game and medicinal plants are commonly accessible to everyone and are not considered to be private property.

Dalits: A broad term for Indigenous Peoples of India, also called "untouchables."

dark energy and *dark matter*: Invisible properties that constitute as much as 95 percent of all that exists.

degrowth movement: Organized and orderly process of winding down human economic activities in order to achieve a level of sustainability.

ecolization: A way of living in which humanity lives in harmony with its environment rather than seeing creation as existing solely for the use of humans, as civilization has done.

Enlightenment: An intellectual movement in Europe that promoted the notion that rational thought provides all of the answers necessary for humanity to survive and prosper.

Good Path: A state of grace that exists when people follow the Creator's original instructions.

Indigenous Eden: The world prior to civilization in which humanity lives in harmony with all created things.

Kise-Manitow: Benevolent Creator; a benevolent Supreme Being who provides the gifts of creation which humans can survive on and learn from.

mosôm: Grandfather; also a term of endearment for male Elders.

nehiyaw: Cree language.

nehiyawak: Cree people.

nehiyaw tapisinowin: The Cree worldview.

original instructions: The instructions received through ceremony that humans are privileged to experience physical life and in return must be grateful and act as stewards of creation.

oskapewis: Ceremonial helper to elders.

Seven Disciplines: Fasting, sharing, parenting, learning, teaching, praying, and meditation, all of which were practiced in order to strengthen spiritual life.

Seven Fires prophecy: It was foretold that strangers who had lost connection with the Good Path would arrive in Turtle Island. If the newcomers do not learn from Indigenous wisdom, there will be a great deal of suffering.

Seven Virtuous Laws (Seven Laws, Seven Virtues): These expectations for harmonious behaviour—humility, honesty, courage, generosity, love, respect, and wisdom—were sacred laws, which, if broken, brought severe repercussions.

spirituality: The belief that there are unseen forces underlying creation, that all created things have spirit, and that humanity experiences life in order to learn, but is not the central focus of creation.

Taoism (Daoism): The Indigenous belief system of China that preceded Confucianism and is still practiced by some.

Tengrism: The Indigenous belief system of the Middle East that has now been almost entirely displaced by Islam.

terra nullius: A legal theory that lands occupied by Indigenous Peoples were not adequately utilized and were consequently considered to be "empty land" and therefore eligible to be claimed by Christian nations.

theory of natural slavery: A theory promoted by Aristotle that peoples who did not think like the Greeks, with their emphasis on the intellect were inferior and could be enslaved.

UNDRIP: The United Nations Declaration on the Rights of Indigenous Peoples, adopted in 2007 with 144 countries voting in favour of the declaration, 4 voting against, and 11 abstaining.

wâhkôhtowin: The importance of positive relationships, especially with the spiritual realm.

wetiko (windigo): The cannibalistic spirit of greed that consumes its victims.

Wîsahkecâhk: A spirit trickster whose purpose was to help humans adapt to earthly life.

wisdom: Intelligence that is guided by spirituality.

BIBLIOGRAPHY

Anderson, Kurt. *Evil Geniuses: The Unmaking of America – A Recent History*. New York: Random House, 2020.

Andros, Michael. *The Church and Indigenous Peoples in the Americas: In Between Reconciliation and Decolonization*. Eugene: Cascade Books, 2019.

Baigent, Michael. *Racing Toward Armageddon: The Three Great Religions and the Plot to End the World*. New York: HarperOne, 2009.

Balsdon, J.P. *Romans and Aliens*. Chapel Hill: University of North Carolina Press, 1979.

Barrat, James. *Our Final Invention: Artificial Intelligence and the End of the Human Era*. New York: St. Martin's Press, 2013.

Benton-Banai, Edward. *The Mishomis Book: The Voice of the Ojibway*. St. Paul: Red School House Publishers, 1988.

Bowden, Brett. *The Empire of Civilization*. Chicago: University of Chicago Press, 2009.

Bruyneel, Kevin. *Settler Memory: The Disavowal of Indigeneity*. Chapel Hill: University of North Carolina Press, 2021.

Cajete, Gregory. *Sacred Journeys: Personal Visions of Transformation.* Vernon: J. Charlton Publishing, 2020.

Canada. Parliament. House of Commons. *Debates,* 5th Parl., 1st Sess., vol. 14 (1883), May 9, 1883.

Careless, J.M.S. *Canada: A Story of Challenge.* Toronto: The MacMillan Company of Canada, 1963.

Cooper, Nancy, and Bradford Keeney, eds. *Shamans of the World.* Boulder: Sounds True, 2008.

Deloria, Vine, Jr. *God is Red.* Golden: North American Press, 1992.

Deloria, Vine, Jr. *The World We Used to Live In.* Golden: Fulcrum Publishing, 2006.

Diamond, Stanley. *In Search of the Primitive: A Critique of Civilization.* New Brunswick, NJ: Transaction Publishers, 2009.

Dillon, Grace, ed. *Walking the Clouds.* Tucson: University of Arizona Press, 2012.

Dunbar-Ortiz, Roxanne. *An Indigenous Peoples' History of the United States.* Boston: Beacon Press, 2014.

Everitt, Anthony. *Alexander the Great: His Life and Mysterious Death.* New York: Random House, 2019.

Feiler, Bruce. *Abraham: A Journey into the Heart of Three Faiths.* New York: Harper Collins, 2004.

Ferguson, Niall. *The Ascent of Money.* New York: Penguin Books, 2018.

Fiola, Chantal. *Rekindling the Sacred Fire.* Winnipeg: University of Manitoba Press, 2015.

Fontaine, Jerry. *Our Hearts Are As One Fire.* Vancouver, BC: UBC Press, 2020.

Forbes, Jack. *Columbus and Other Cannibals.* New York: Seven Stories Press, 2008.

Ghosh, Amitav. *The Nutmeg's Curse*. Chicago: University of Illinois Press, 2021.

Goldstein, Jacob. *Money: The True Story of a Made-Up Thing*. New York: Hachette Books, 2020.

Graeber, David, and David Wengrow. *The Dawn of Everything*. London: Penguin Random House, 2021.

Hariri, Yuval Noah. *Sapiens: A Brief History of Mankind*. Toronto: McClelland & Stewart, 2014.

Harner, Michael. *The Way of the Shaman*. New York: Harper & Row, 1990.

Johnson, Basil. *Ojibway Heritage*. Toronto: McClelland and Stewart, 1976.

Kallis, Giorgos, Susan Paulson, Giacomo D'Alisa, and Federico Demaria. *The Case for Degrowth*. Cambridge: Polity Press, 2001.

Katz, Richard. *Indigenous Healing Psychology*. Toronto: Healing Arts Press, 2017.

Kirkland, Russell. *Taoism: The Enduring Tradition*. New York: Routledge, 2004.

Khan, Ali. *The Next Pandemic*. New York: Hachette Books, 2020.

Kohn, Livia. *Daoism and Chinese Culture*. St. Petersburg, FL: Three Pines Press, 2001.

Kulchyski, Peter, Don McCaskill, and David Newhouse, eds. *In the Words of Elders*. Toronto: University of Toronto Press, 1999.

Levinson, Jon. *Inheriting Abraham: The Legacy of the Patriarch in Judaism, Christianity and Islam*. Princeton: Princeton University Press, 2012.

Mails, Thomas. *Fools Crow: Wisdom and Power*. Skiatook: Tri S Foundation, 2001.

Marais, Julian. *History of Philosophy*. Garden City, NY: Dover Publications, 1967.

McAdam, Sylvia. *Nationhood Interrupted: Revitalizing nehiyaw Legal Systems*. Saskatoon: Purich Publishing, 2015.

McIntyre, Lee. *Post-Truth*. Cambridge, MA: MIT Press, 2018.

McKibben, Bill. *Falter: Has the Human Game Begun to Play Itself Out?* New York: Henry Holt, 2019.

Meili, Dianne. *Those Who Know: Profile of Alberta's Aboriginal Elders*. Edmonton: NeWest Publishers, 2012.

Miller, James. *Daoism*. Oxford: Oneworld Publications, 2003.

Miller, James. *Shingwauk's Vision: A History of Native Residential Schools*. Toronto: University of Toronto Press, 1996.

Nadeau, Denise. *Unsettling Spirit: A Journey into Decolonization*. Montreal and Kingston: McGill-Queen's University Press, 2020.

Napoleon, Art. "Key Terms and Concepts for Exploring Nîhiyaw Tâpisinowin the Cree Worldview." Master's thesis, University of Victoria, 2014.

Neihardt, John. *Black Elk Speaks*. Lincoln: University of Nebraska Press, 1979.

Nelson, Melissa. *Original Instructions: Indigenous Teachings for a Sustainable Future*. Rochester: Bear & Company, 2008.

Olupona, Jacob. *African Religions*. New York: Oxford University Press, 2014.

Orrell, David, and Roman Chlupaty. *The Evolution of Money*. New York: Columbia University Press, 2016.

Pearcey, Mark. *The Exclusions of Civilization: Indigenous Peoples in the Story of International Society*. New York: Palgrave Macmillan, 2016.

Peat, David. *Blackfoot Physics*. Boston: Weiser Books, 2005.

Potter, Andrew. *On Decline*. Windsor, ON: Biblioasis, 2021.

Postman, Neil. *Amusing Ourselves to Death*. New York: Penguin Books, 1985.

Postman, Neil. *The End of Education*. New York: Vintage Books, 1995.

Qualman, Darrin. *Civilization Critical: Energy, Food, Nature and the Future*. Black Point, NS: Fernwood, 2019.

Redvers, Nicole. *The Science of the Sacred*. Berkeley, CA: North Atlantic Books, 2019.

Rice, Brian. *Seeing the World with Aboriginal Eyes*. Winnipeg: Aboriginal Issues Press, 2005.

Ryan, Christopher. *Civilized to Death*. New York: Simon and Schuster, 2019.

Sala, Enric. *The Nature of Nature: Why We Need the Wild*. Washington: National Geographic, 2020.

Sammel, Alison. *Indigenizing Education*. Singapore: Springer, 2020.

Saskatchewan Ministry of Education. "Renewed Objectives for the Common Essential Learnings of Critical and Creative Thinking and Personal and Social Development." Regina: Saskatchewan Ministry of Education, 2008.

Saul, John Ralston. *The Unconscious Civilization*. Concord, ON: House of Anansi Press, 1995.

Schroeter, John. *After Shock*. Bainbridge Island, WA: Abundant World Institute, 2020.

Some, Malidoma Patrice. *The Healing Wisdom of Africa*. New York: Penguin Putnam, 1998.

Stonechild, Blair. *The Knowledge Seeker*. Regina: University of Regina Press, 2016.

Stonechild, Blair. *Loss of Indigenous Eden and the Fall of Spirituality*. Regina: University of Regina Press, 2020.

Stonechild, Blair. *The New Buffalo: The Struggle for Aboriginal Post-Secondary Education in Canada*. Winnipeg: University of Manitoba Press, 2006.

Stonechild, Blair, and Sharlene McGowan. "More Holistic Assessment for Improved Education Outcomes." Regina: Saskatchewan Instructional Development and Research Unit, University of Regina, 2009.

Storm, Hyemeyohsts. *Seven Arrows*. New York: Ballantyne Books, 1972.

Suzuki, David. *The Sacred Balance*. Vancouver: Greystone Books, 2007.

Truth and Reconciliation Commission of Canada. *Truth and Reconciliation Commission of Canada: Calls to Action*. Winnipeg: Truth and Reconciliation Commission of Canada, 2015.

Wallace-Wells, David. *The Uninhabitable Earth: Life After Warming*. New York: Tim Duggan Books, 2020.

Weatherford, Jack. *Indian Givers*. New York: Fawcett Columbine, 1988.

Weatherford, Jack. *Savages and Civilization: Who Will Survive?* New York: Ballantine Books, 1995.

Williams, Robert, Jr. *Savage Anxieties: The Invention of Western Civilization*. New York: Palgrave Macmillan, 2012.

Wolf, Eric. *Europe and the People Without History*. Berkeley, CA: University of California Press, 2010.

Zerzan, John, ed. *Against Civilization: Readings and Reflections*. Port Townsend, WA: Feral House, 2005.

Zerzan, John. *A People's History of Civilization*. Port Townsend, WA: Feral House, 2018.

NOTES

1 "Oxford Languages and Google," *OxfordLanguages*, accessed July 9, 2021, https://languages.oup.com/google-dictionary-en.

2 I cover Danny Musqua's life and teachings in my book *The Knowledge Seeker: Embracing Indigenous Spirituality* (Regina: University of Regina, 2016), 43–90. Mosôm Danny passed into the spirit world on December 5, 2022.

3 Stonechild, *The Knowledge Seeker*, 45.

4 Genesis 2:16–17 (New International Version).

5 Stonechild, *The Knowledge Seeker*, 162–3.

6 Stonechild, *The Knowledge Seeker*, 162–3. The book *Amerindian Rebirth: Reincarnation Belief among North American Indians and Inuit* (Toronto: University of Toronto Press, 1994), edited by Antonia Mills and Richard Slobodin, reveals that beliefs in rebirth are widespread among Indigenous Peoples. Some features general to the recall of previous lives by young children include their insistence on having lived the former life and providing details that are often confirmed through independent research. Among the children who claimed to have died violently, many bear birthmarks that closely resemble relevant wounds, such as those created by a bullet or knife.

7 *Homo sapiens sapiens* means "wise ones."

8 Stonechild, *The Knowledge Seeker*, 52.

9 The prevalence of star origin stories is discussed in my book *Loss of Indigenous Eden and the Fall of Spirituality* (Regina: University of Regina

Press, 2020). Sacred stories regarding matters such as our origins were told according to age and interest. Wîsahkecâhk stories, often involving animals and illustrating lessons learned though mishaps, are popular for children. Stories like The Rolling Head, which is a type of origin story, explain why various geographic features arose and could satisfy an adolescent audience. The purpose of such myths was not to be rational or factual descriptions, but rather to inspire a sense of awe, respect, and humility towards creation. Other than carrying out their responsibilities to care for and nurture creation, Indigenous Peoples had faith in the benevolence of the Creator and did not perceive a need to take over management of everything. More advanced discussions of origins, such as star stories, occurred in ceremonial contexts and delved into deeper revelations such as our nature as spirit beings and our journey in coming to Earth.

10   Canada, Parliament, House of Commons, *Debates*, 5th Parl., 1st Sess., vol. 14 (1883), May 9, 1883: 1107–8.

11   James Miller, *Shingwauk's Vision: A History of Native Residential Schools* (Toronto: University of Toronto Press, 1996), 133.

12   Statement of Pope Francis at Maskwachis First Nation, Canada, July 25, 2022.

13   Stonechild, *The Knowledge Seeker*, 43–90. Ernest was one of the first Elders I met when I began teaching at First Nations University of Canada (then Saskatchewan Indian Federated College) in 1977. Ernest was also interviewed by Roy Bonisteel of CBC on the concept of Indigenous Eden.

14   Ernest Tootootsis, personal communication. Tootoosis also spoke about not abusing the Garden of Eden.

15   Stonechild, *Loss of Indigenous Eden*, 70.

16   See the discussion of the emergence of civilization in Chapter 3 of my book *Loss of Indigenous Eden*, 63–92.

17   Sylvia McAdam, *Nationhood Interrupted: Revitalizing nehiyaw Legal Systems* (Saskatoon: Purich Publishing, 2015), 38.

18   Richard Katz, *Indigenous Healing Psychology* (Toronto: Healing Arts Press, 2017), 180.

19   "What Is Paganism?," Papal Apology Project (1999), 3.

20   Marlene Laurelle, "Religious Revival, Nationalism and the Invention of Tradition: Political Tengrism in Central Asia and Tatarstan," *Central Asia Survey* 26, no. 2 (2007): 203–16.

21   M.C. Raj, "Cosmosity: Dalits and the Spirituality of the Commons,"
      Vocabulary Commons, accessed August 3, 2022, https://wiki.p2pfoundation
      .net/Dalits_and_the_Spirituality_of_the_Commons.
22   Raj, "Cosmosity."
23   John Zerzan, *A People's History of Civilization* (Port Townsend, WA: Feral
      House, 2018), 120.
24   International Commission for a History of the Scientific and Cultural
      Development of Mankind, *History of Mankind: Cultural and Scientific
      Development and the Beginnings of Civilization*, vol. 1 (London: George
      Allen and Unwin, 1965), 4.
25   International Commission, *History of Mankind*, 8.
26   Zerzan, *A People's History of Civilization*, 49.
27   Population figures gleaned from the following sources: Colin McEvedy
      and Richard Jones, *Atlas of World Population History* (New York: Facts
      on File, 1978); John Durand, "Historical Estimates of World Population:
      An Evaluation" (Philadelphia: Population Studies Center, University of
      Pennsylvania, 1974); and Angus Maddison, *The World Economy: Historical
      Statistics*, vol. 2 (Paris: OECD, 2003).
28   "Hammurabi's Code: An Eye for an Eye," *Ancient Civilizations*, accessed
      October 21, 2018, http://www.ushistory.org/civ/4c.asp.
29   Julian Marais, *History of Philosophy* (New York: Dover Publications, 1967), 37.
30   Cited in Nicholas Smith, "Aristotle's Theory of Slavery," *Phoenix* 37, no. 2
      (July 1983), accessed April 2, 2019, https://www.researchgate.net
      /publication/269874483_Aristotle's_Theory_of_Natural_Slavery.
31   Cited in Smith, "Aristotle's Theory of Slavery," 80.
32   Stonechild, *Loss of Indigenous Eden*, 54–5.
33   J.P. Balsdon, *Romans and Aliens* (Chapel Hill: University of North Carolina
      Press, 1979), 4.
34   The episode "Boudica's Revenge" in the *Eight Days That Made Rome*
      television series describes derogatory Roman attitudes towards the
      Indigenous Peoples of Britain.
35   John Mohawk, "The Art of Thriving in Place," in Melissa K. Nelson,
      ed., *Original Instructions: Indigenous Teachings for a Sustainable Future*
      (Rochester: Bear & Company, 2008): 126–36.
36   Christopher Ryan, *Civilized to Death* (New York: Simon and Schuster,
      2019), 14.

37 Ryan, *Civilized to Death*, 10–11

38 Ryan, *Civilized to Death*, 41–2.

39 Ryan, *Civilized to Death*, 61.

40 Douglas Fry, *War, Peace and Human Nature* (Oxford: Oxford University Press, 2015), cited in Ryan, *Civilized to Death*, 96.

41 "China's Population: Issues and Trends in China's Demographic History," *Asia for Educators*, accessed May 30, 2023, www.afe.easia.columbia.edu.

42 Aaron O'Neil, "Population of India from 1800 to 2020," Statista, June 21, 2022, accessed May 23, 2023, www.Statista.com.

43 Jack Weatherford, *Indian Givers* (New York: Ballentine Books, 1989), 63, 71.

44 Ryan, *Civilized to Death*, 10.

45 Ryan, *Civilized to Death*, 67.

46 Leviathan XIII.9, quoted in Ryan, *Civilized to Death*, 69.

47 "History of Slavery," *Wikipedia*, accessed June 24, 2022, https://en.wikipedia.org/wiki/History_of_slavery.

48 Levi Ricket, "U.S. Presidents in Their Own Words Concerning American Indians," *Native News Online*, February 20, 2023, accessed May 15, 2023, www.nativenewsonline.net.

49 Michael Crosby, "Assault on a Sacred Place," *Common Edge*, accessed April 10, 2022, https://commonedge.org/assault-on-a-sacred-place.

50 Tadiski Dozono, "Indigenous Epistemic Interventions for State Curriculum: Moving Beyond the Abrahamic Covenant of Manifest Destiny," in Abdou Ehaab and Theodore Zervas, *Historical and Living Indigenous Wisdom Traditions in Curricula and Textbooks* (Toronto: University of Toronto Press, forthcoming 2024).

51 Tina Butler, "Pre-Columbian Amazon Supported Millions of People," *Mongabay*, accessed September 16, 2022, https://news.mongabay.com/2005/10/pre-columbian-amazon-supported-millions-of-people/.

52 Katie Surma, "Bolsonaro Should Be Tried for Crimes Against Humanity, Indigenous Leaders Say," accessed October 21, 2021, nbcnews.com.

53 Surma, "Bolsonaro should be tried...".

54 Nicholas Kusnetz, "From Chernobyl to the Amazon: Inside the Growing Movement to Criminalize 'Ecocide,'" Inside Climate News, June 24, 2021, accessed October 2, 2022, InsideClimateNews.org.

55 "Indigenous Tribes Accuse President Bolsonaro of Genocide at The Hague," *Euronews*, October 21, 2021.

56   This expression comes from E.R. Wolf, *Europe and the People Without History* (Berkeley: University of California Press, 1982), 127.

57   Dictionary.com, s.v. "wisdom," accessed August 16, 2020.

58   Art Napoleon, "Key Terms and Concepts for Exploring Nîhiyaw Tâpisinowin the Cree Worldview" (master's thesis, University of Victoria, 2014), 18.

59   Napoleon, "Key Terms and Concepts", 21

60   Napoleon, "Key Terms and Concepts", 61, 72.

61   Southern Dictionary, cited in Napoleon, 34.

62   Online Etymology Dictionary, s.v. "God", accessed May 16, 2022, https://www.etymonline.com/word/god.

63   Neil Postman, *Amusing Ourselves to Death* (New York: Penguin Books, 1985), 71–2.

64   Postman, *Amusing Ourselves to Death*, 78.

65   Postman, *Amusing Ourselves to Death*, 16.

66   Postman, *Amusing Ourselves to Death*, 97.

67   Postman, *Amusing Ourselves to Death*, 126.

68   Postman, *Amusing Ourselves to Death*, 106.

69   Postman, *Amusing Ourselves to Death*, 155–6.

70   Genesis 2:17 (New International Version).

71   "Lion People of the Kalahari," *Tribes, Predators & Me*, Series 1, Episode 2, British Broadcasting Corporation, October 2020.

72   Stonechild, *Loss of Indigenous Eden*, 41.

73   Jacob Goldstein. *Money: The True Story of a Made-Up Thing* (New York: Hachette Books, 2020), 9.

74   Goldstein, *Money*, 16–18.

75   Goldstein, *Money*, 80.

76   Goldstein, *Money*, 79.

77   Goldstein, *Money*, 88.

78   Giorgos Kallis, Susan Paulson, Giacomo D'Alisa, and Federico Demaria, *The Case for Degrowth* (Cambridge: Polity Press, 2001), 12.

79   Goldstein, *Money*, 192.

80   Goldstein, *Money*, 207.

81   Goldstein, *Money*, 212.

82   To understand the depths and depravity to which civilization can sink, one need merely look at the Roman Empire and its treatment of the Indigenous Peoples of Europe or, for a more recent example, Nazi

Germany, with its concept of racial superiority, determined to dominate and even eradicate what were perceived as inferior races, with the ultimate goal being the total acquisition of wealth and power, the distinguishing characteristics of civilization.

83   Stonechild, *Loss of Indigenous Eden*, 181.

84   Rebecca Shaw, "68% Average Decline in Species Population Sizes since 1970," *World Wildlife Organization*, September 9, 2020, accessed July 31, 2022, https://www.worldwildlife.org/press-releases/68-average-decline -in-species-population-sizes-since-1970-says-new-wwf-report.

85   James Barrat, *Our Final Invention: Artificial Intelligence and the End of the Human Era* (New York: St. Martin's Press, 2013), 235.

86   Barrat, *Our Final Invention*, 241.

87   Barrat, *Our Final Invention*, 236.

88   David Wallace-Wells, *The Uninhabitable Earth: Life After Warming* (New York: Tim Duggan Books, 2020), 8.

89   Wallace-Wells, *The Uninhabitable Earth*, 104–6.

90   Wallace-Wells, *The Uninhabitable Earth*, 63.

91   Wallace-Wells, *The Uninhabitable Earth*, 146.

92   Wallace-Wells, *The Uninhabitable Earth*, 36.

93   Wallace-Wells, *The Uninhabitable Earth*, 38.

94   Wallace-Wells, *The Uninhabitable Earth*, 220.

95   Julian Marais, *History of Philosophy* (Garden City, NY: Dover Publications, 1967), 10–14.

96   Bruce Feiler, *Abraham: A Journey to the Heart of Three Faiths* (New York: Harper Collins, 2004), 19.

97   Feiler, *Abraham*, 13.

98   Feiler, *Abraham*, 33.

99   Feiler, *Abraham*, 30.

100 Robert Williams Jr., *Savage Anxieties: The Invention of Western Civilization* (New York: Palgrave Macmillan, 2012), 5.

101 Williams, *Savage Anxieties*, 29.

102 Williams, *Savage Anxieties*, 96.

103 Williams, *Savage Anxieties*, 122–4.

104 Williams, *Savage Anxieties*, 216.

105 *Encyclopedia Britannica*, s.v. "Cogito ergo sum," accessed December 2, 2018, www.britannica.com.

106 Peter Kulchyski, Don McCaskill, and David Newhouse, eds., *In the Words of Elders* (Toronto: University of Toronto Press, 1999), 56.
107 Dictionary.com, s.v. "Knowledge," accessed November 23, 2018, www.dictionary.com.
108 Oxford Dictionaries, s.v. "Science", accessed February 22, 2019, www.oxforddictionaries.com.
109 Zerzan, *A People's History of Civilization*, 250.
110 Katz, *Indigenous Healing Psychology*, 167.
111 Katz, *Indigenous Healing Psychology*, 176.
112 Katz, *Indigenous Healing Psychology*, 172.
113 Katz, *Indigenous Healing Psychology*, 202.
114 Katz, *Indigenous Healing Psychology*, 276.
115 Katz, *Indigenous Healing Psychology*, 312.
116 Katz, *Indigenous Healing Psychology*, 385.
117 Helen Dukas and Banesh Hoffman, eds., *Albert Einstein, The Human Side: New Glimpses from His Archives* (Princeton: Princeton University Press, 1981), 32–33.
118 Vine Deloria Jr., *The World We Used to Live In* (Golden: Fulcrum Publishing, 2006), 46, 50–3, 57–62, 76–81, 107–22, 125–30, 139–40, and 144–7.
119 Deloria, *The World We Used to Live In*, 91.
120 In his book *Spirit Talkers*, anthropologist William Lyon, who studies such phenomena, is convinced that Indigenous Peoples had discovered such a methodology. He also notes that as the Indigenous world unravelled, fewer and fewer were able to serve as practitioners, causing this set of knowledge and skills to dramatically fade.
121 See Chapter 6, "Knowledge Sacred and Profane," 159–77.
122 Ryan, *Civilized to Death*, 38.
123 Richard Dawkins, *The Selfish Gene* (Oxford: Oxford University Press, 1976).
124 Dawkins, *The Selfish Gene*, 39.
125 Christopher Klein, "DNA Study Finds Aboriginal Australians World's Oldest Civilization," *History*, August 22, 2018, accessed September 16, 2022, https://www.history.com/news/dna-study-finds-aboriginal-australians-worlds-oldest-civilization.
126 Father Hugonard, who founded the Qu'Appelle Indian Residential School I attended, saw no place for Indigenous music and dance: "The change from discipline and a regular life to unbridled license and debauchery

soon transform a promising youth into a shiftless unreliable Indian...
nearly nude, painted and decked out in feathers and beads, dancing
like demented individuals.... I am convinced that Christianity and
advancement and paganism and indolence cannot flourish side by side.
One or the other has to give way; paganism, dancing and indolence are
the most natural to the Indian, who has no thought for the morrow."
Quoted in Brian Titley, *A Narrow Vision: Duncan Campbell Scott and the
Administration of Indian Affairs in Canada* (Vancouver, BC: University of
British Columbia Press, 1986), 169.

127 Ryan, *Civilized to Death*, 64, 175.

128 Deloria, *The World We Used to Live In*, 83–105.

129 Stonechild, *The Knowledge Seeker*, 43–67.

130 Stonechild, *The Knowledge Seeker*, 69–90.

131 Arthur Ray, *Indians in the Fur Trade* (Toronto: University of Toronto Press,
1974).

132 Stonechild, *The Knowledge Seeker*, 69–90.

133 Katz, *Indigenous Healing Psychology*, 117–68.

134 Stonechild, *Loss of Indigenous Eden*, 179–99.

135 Wikipedia, s.v. "African elephant," accessed March 3, 2022, www.wikipedia
.org.

136 "Life in Balance," *WikiPop*, accessed July 7, 2022, http://www.Wikipop.org.

137 "Historic vs Present Geographical Distribution of Lions," *Brilliant Maps*,
April 26, 2016, accessed March 3, 2022, https://brilliantmaps.com/?s=lions.

138 James Macdonald, "The Downside of Renewable Energy," *JSTOR Daily*,
May 6, 2019, accessed September 16, 2022, https://daily.jstor.org/the
-downside-to-renewable-energy/.

139 Max Roser, Hannah Ritchie, Eteban Ortiz-Ospina, and Lucas Rodés-
Guirao, "World Population Growth," *Our World in Data*, accessed June 3,
2023, https://ourworldindata.org/world-population-growth.

140 Deena Robinson, "25 Facts About Food Waste," *Earth.org*, February 3, 2002,
accessed July 31, 2022, https://earth.org/facts-about-food-waste/.

141 "China's Indigenous Religion: Taoism Emphasizes Harmony between
Humanity and Nature," *CGTN*, accessed June 5, 2023, https://news.cgtn
.com/news/3341544f34494464776c6d636a4e6e62684a4856/index.html.

142 Chris B. Murphy, "What Is the Rule of 70?" *Investopedia*, accessed April 19,
2023, https://www.investopedia.com/terms/r/rule-of-70.asp.

143 Kallis et al., *The Case for Degrowth*, 26.

144 Kallis et al., 28–9.

145 The degrowth movement is led by groups such as Research & Degrowth – Barcelona and has a global network. The movement is sometimes wrongly criticized as a threat to economic prosperity.

146 Kallis et al., xiv.

147 Kallis et al., 46.

148 Kallis et al., 18.

149 Kallis et al., 60.

150 Kallis et al., 48.

151 Kallis et al., 91.

152 Kallis et al., 106.

153 Malidoma Some, *The Healing Wisdom of Africa* (New York: Penguin Putnam, 1999), 2.

154 Napoleon, "Key Terms and Concepts," 91.

155 United Nations Department of Economic and Social Affairs, "United Nations Declaration on the Rights of Indigenous Peoples—Historical Overview," accessed March 22, 2019, www.un.org/development/desa.

156 "Bolivia Enshrines Natural World's Rights with Equal Status for Mother Earth," *The Guardian*, April 10, 2011, accessed July 8, 2022, https://www.theguardian.com/environment/2011/apr/10/bolivia-enshrines-natural-world-rights.

157 The figure 800,000 years is based upon the estimate that primate species should persist for 1,000,000 years. So far, modern humans have existed for 200,000 years. "The Current Mass Extinction," PBS, accessed August 10, 2019, https://www.pbs.org/wgbh/evolution/library/03/2/l_032_04.html.

158 John Shroeter, *After Shock* (Bainbridge Island, WA: Abundant World Institute, 2020), 458.

159 Shroeter, *After Shock*, 435.

160 Shroeter, *After Shock*, 447.

161 Shroeter, *After Shock*, 299.

162 Shroeter, *After Shock*, 307.

163 Shroeter, *After Shock*, 505, 513.

164 Shroeter, *After Shock*, 508.

165 I testified in the Ochapowace Tax Case mounted by the Ochapowace First Nation in 2000. Their Elders provided testimony about their people's

long existence on the land prior to European contact and that they never surrendered or agreed to give up their sovereignty. The First Nation argued that for this reason their own sovereign rights need to be recognized presently. This case directly challenged the concept of *terra nullius* and the idea that a foreign state that had never stepped foot on the land should be able to assume ownership over everything, including the inhabitants, lock, stock, and barrel. The judge did not take Ochapowace's argument very seriously and simply dismissed the Elders' arguments. The case would have put in danger the principle that enables Canada and other nations to exist in their current state.

166 Danny Musqua, interview with author, First Nations University, Saskatoon Campus, April 9, 2012.

167 Danny Musqua, interview with author, First Nations University, Saskatoon Campus, October 24, 2012.

168 "Billions of Earth-like Planets in Milky Way," CBC, accessed November 4, 2013, http://www.cbc.ca/news/technology/billions-of-earth-like-planets -in-milky -way-study-1.2356237.

169 Prophecy of the Seven Fires as related in Sherry Mitchell, *Sacred Instructions: Indigenous Wisdom for Living Spirit-Based Change* (Berkeley, CA: North Atlantic Books, Berkeley, 2018), 221–4.

INDEX

epidemics, 86, 125, 126, 133
ethics, 62

faith: science and, 113
"fake news," 62
fasting, 130
Feiler, Bruce: *Abraham: A Journey to the Heart of Three Faiths*, 97
fine arts, 109
First Nations University of Canada, 1, 153, 194n13
foraging way of life, 35–36
forest fires, 91
fossil fuel industry, 92
Francis, Pope, 7–8, 54, 156, 168
freedom: concept of, 51
free speech, 52
futurists, 163–64

General Electric, 79
generosity: virtue of, xii, 11, 13, 103, 172
geography, 99, 108–9
giraffes, 132
God: concepts of, 65–66, 96–97
Goldstein, Jacob: *Money: The True Story of a Made-Up Thing*, 78, 79, 82
Good Path, xi, 184
Gordon, Theodore, 163
Great Britain: colonialism of, 44–45, 80; economy of, 79; privatization of the commons, 80
"Great Law of Peace," 104
"Great Nutrient Collapse," 91–92
greed, xiv, xv, 70–71, 133, 171, 173
Greek culture: abandonment of humility, 29–30, 96; disrespect

of barbarians, 97–98; exceptionalism of, 27; as recent past, 123; slavery, 28–29
green technology, 134

Haudenosaunee, 104
Hawking, Stephen, 172
health and wellness: Indigenous approaches to, 124–26
herbal medicines, 111
Herodotus, 106
history: bias of, 107; Indigenous and non-Indigenous approaches to, x, 21–22, 106–7; progress and, 22
Hobbes, Thomas, 31, 44, 140
Holy Roman Empire: expansion of, 31–32
homo sapiens sapiens, 4, 24, 193n7
honesty: virtue of, xii–xiii, 11, 62, 172, 174
Hudson's Bay Company, 79, 125
Hugonard, Father, 199n126
humanism, 99
humanity: dangerous trajectory of, 137–38, 162; period of survival of, 169, 201n157; predictions about the future of, 144, 163–64, 176–77
humans: Greek philosophers on, 96; nature and, 69–70, 96; origin and evolution of, 4, 13, 24–25, 70, 175, 193n9; relationship with plants and animals, 25, 76, 96; selfishness of, 115; as spirit being, 4–5, 175; as stewards of creation, 131
human sacrifice, 29, 32, 46, 104

knowledge: definition of, 104–5; Indigenous perspective on, 73; production of, 60–61; vs. wisdom, 59
Knowledge Seeker: Embracing Indigenous Spirituality, The (Stonechild), ix, ix–x, 8, 62, 114

lacrosse, 121
land: boundaries, 133; non-Indigenous exploration of, 129–30, 153; sacred relationship to, 15, 48, 129
lions, 31, 76, 132
Loss of Indigenous Eden (Stonechild), ix, x, 9, 24, 60, 114
love: virtue of, 11, 13, 30, 172
Lyon, William: *Spirit Talkers*, 199n120
Lyons, Oren, 165

Manifest Destiny, 50–51
mathematics, 45, 59–60, 99, 154
Mayan culture, 14–15, 28, 39
media: commercialization of, 68
mental wellness, 92–93, 115, 126–27
metallurgy, 69
Metuktire, Raoni, 54, 55
Middle East: Indigenous Peoples of, 16–17
Mills, Antonia, 193n6; *Amerindian Rebirth*, 3
mind. *See* intellect
Mohawk, John, 34
money: as artificial economy, 81–82; impact on social relationships, 79, 108, 145–46; Indigenous society and, 60, 108, 147; invention of,

78–79; pop culture and, 120; value of, 81–82; virtual, 82–83
Money: The True Story of a Made-Up Thing (Goldstein), 78
Morales, Evo, 157
mosôm (Grandfather), 1, 2, 175, 176, 184
Mother Earth, 22, 158
Muscowpetung First Nation, 47
music, 119–20
Musk, Elon, 155, 172
Musqua, Danny: on communist countries, 138; education of, 10; on Indigenous spirituality, 110, 111; on origin of humanity, 174; out-of-body experience of, 4; on space travel, 156, 176–77; teachings of, ix, 1, 2

Napoleon, Art, 114, 155; "Key Terms and Concepts for Exploring Nîhiyaw Tâpisinowin, the Cree Worldview," 63
national borders, 44
natural vs. artificial, 75
nature: as authentic base of life, xiii, 75; civilization and, xii, 23, 24, 33–34, 77, 102; human relationships with, 69–70, 148–49; Indigenous relationships with, 33–34, 75–76, 102, 130, 162–63; non-Indigenous view of, 76; as nurture, 76–77; spiritual side of, 165–66; technological impacts on, 87, 147–48
Nazi Germany: concept of racial superiority, 198n82

Blair Stonechild is a member of the Muscowpetung First Nation in Saskatchewan. He is a residential school survivor and was the first faculty member hired at the First Nations University of Canada in 1976. He is an author of five previous books and lives in Regina with his wife Sylvia and three adult children.